SUMERIAN RECORDS FROM DREHEM

COLUMBIA UNIVERSITY ORIENTAL STUDIES

Vol. VIII

SUMERIAN RECORDS FROM DREHEM

BY

WILLIAM M. NESBIT

AMS PRESS, INC.

NEW YORK, N.Y. 10003

1966

NOTE

The business and record literature of early Babylonia has asumed such extensive proportions that it now constitutes a disinct branch of Assyriology in itself. The thousands of tablets mbodying business documents of all sorts, such as Temple records, deeds of sale, public and private contracts, etc., are often more important for the study of the religious and social life of he Babylonians than detailed historical records. Although peraps less interesting to the modern reader than pure history, these drily-expressed and often abbreviated documents give an admirable picture of the daily life and hence of the social culture of the civilization where they originated.

In the following volume, Dr. Nesbit presents an exhaustive treatise on thirty tablets from Drehem now in his possession, which belong under the classification of business documents, some being lists of live stock, intended both for the Temples and individuals, others being invoices for deliveries of property. Inasmuch as the language of these records is purely Sumerian, although used, as Dr. Nesbit points out, in a closely abbreviated style, they are of peculiar interest to the investigator of ancient Sumerian forms. Dating from a period slightly earlier than the twenty-fourth century B.C., this literature indicates a remarkably high grade of commercial development in what was probably a non-Semitic community.

Dr. Nesbit has succeeded in obtaining satisfactory renderings for almost every line and in some instances has offered new solutions of the intricacies of this very difficult form of text.

JOHN DYNELEY PRINCE

COLUMBIA UNIVERSITY

v

INSCRIBED TO

THEODORA BENEDICT DENNIS

Šarrat Libbia

PREFACE

The period of the hegemony of the city of Ur over the land which a later age has denominated "Babylonia" was characterized by a very high grade of civilization. The numerous contemporary records which have come to light within the last few years indicate this in no uncertain way. The most recent discovery of these documents is the rich store found by the natives at Drehem, and smuggled by them out of the country; of which find the tablets described in this book are a part.

Special attention has been given herein to the detailed study of the peculiar jargon in which these ancient business records were written. Moreover each tablet has been illustrated, transliterated, and translated, in full; so that the entire process of decipherment may be followed out step for step. So although these thirty tablets do not contain much material that is entirely new, it is hoped that the method of handling may be of interest to the student of this class of literature.

I wish at this time to acknowledge my indebtedness to Professor John Dyneley Prince of Columbia University, without whose kindly cooperation as teacher and friend this monograph would have been impossible. I desire also to express my profound gratitude to Professor Robert William Rogers of Drew Theological Seminary, who first aroused in me an interest in the study of the ancient Orient, and whose friendship and interest have been a constant stimulus in my work. To Professor Richard J. H. Gottheil of Columbia University many thanks are due for numerous helpful suggestions and especially for having proposed the theme of this dissertation. Finally to Dr. Frederick A. Vanderburgh, untiring student of Assyriology, I am deeply indebted. He has carefully gone over all the translations and has furnished very material assistance with some difficult renderings. In particular, his familiarity with the old Babylonian seals was of great advantage to me.

Of course, it is needless for any student of Assyriology to mention his dependence upon Brünnow's *Sign-List* and Delitzsch's *Lesestücke;* but I wish to place alongside these books, as having been invaluable to me in this study, *Old Babylonian Temple Records* by my friend Dr. Robert J. Lau, and Prince's *Materials for a Sumerian Lexicon.* I have also derived much help from Langdon's *Sumerian Grammar*, King's *History of Sumer and Akkad*, Legrain's *Le Temps des Rois d'Ur*, and Barton's *Babylonian Writing.*

W. M. N.

MONTCLAIR, N. J.,
June 1, 1914.

TABLE OF CONTENTS

LIST OF ABBREVIATIONS AND GRAPHIC
CHARACTERS EMPLOYED IN THE BOOK

Abbreviations

AJSL	= American Journal of Semitic Languages and Literatures.
AL[5]	= Delitzsch; Assyrische Lesestücke (Fünfte Auflage).
BA	= Beiträge zur Assyriologie.
BE	= The Babylonian Expedition of the University of Pennsylvania, edited by H. V. Hilprecht.
BE, XIV	= Clay; Documents from the Temple Archives of Nippur, Dated in the Reigns of Cassite Rulers (Complete Dates)—BE. Series A. Volume XIV.
BE, XV	= Clay; Documents from the Temple Archives of Nippur, Dated in the Reigns of Cassite Rulers (Incomplete Dates)—BE. Series A. Volume XV.
Br	= Brünnow; Classified List of all simple and compound cuneiform ideographs.
BSO	= Barton; A Sketch of Semitic Origins.
BBW	= Barton; Babylonian Writing.
CT	= Cuneiform Texts in the British Museum, copied by Pinches, King, and Thompson.
EBH	= Radau; Early Babylonian History.
GTD	= de Genouillac; Tablettes de Drehem.
HBA	= Rogers; History of Babylonia and Assyria.
HSA	= King; History of Sumer and Akkad.
ISA	= Thureau-Dangin; Inscriptions Sumeriennes Archaiques.
JAOS	= Journal of the American Oriental Society.

JBL = Journal of Biblical Literature.

KAT = Schrader; Die Keilenschriften und das Alt Testament.

LSG = Langdon; Sumerian Grammar.

M-A = Muss-Arnold; Concise Dictionary of the Assyrian Language.

MSL = Prince; Materials for a Sumerian Lexicon.

OBTR = Lau; Old Babylonian Temple Records.

PAAB = Halévy; Précis d'Allographie Assyro-Babylonienne.

PN = Peters; Nippur.

RBBA = Jastrow; Religious Belief in Babylonia and Assyria.

Rec. Trav. = Thureau-Dangin; Recueil de Travaux relatifs à la Philologie Égyptienne et Assyrienne.

RA = Revue d'Assyriologie.

SAD = Myhrmann; Sumerian Administrative Documents. —BE. Series A. Volume III. Part I.

SAI = Meissner; Seltene Assyrische Ideogramme.

TAD = Langdon; Tablets from the Archives of Drehem.

TRU = Legrain; Le Temps des Rois d'Ur.

Other abbreviations used are obvious.

GRAPHIC CHARACTERS

x = Semitic ח

q = Semitic ק

c = Semitic צ

š = Semitic שׁ

PART I

INTRODUCTORY MATTER

§ 1. HISTORICAL SKETCH

The dawn of history finds the lower plain of the Tigris and the Euphrates occupied by two distinct races. A non-Semitic people, now known as the Sumerians, predominated in the southern portion of the country; while in the north the power was in the hands of a Semitic stock, called by us the Babylonians or Akkadians, but seemingly self-described as "the black-headed people." In the South, which came ultimately to be called "the Land of Sumer (or Shumer),"were the great cities of Lagash (Shirpurla), Ur, Erech, Gishuch (Umma), and Eridu; and in the North, which at a later time was distinguished as "the Land of Akkad," were the strongholds of Kish, Agade (from which "Akkad" took its name), Sippar, and Babylon. It is generally agreed that the Sumerians were the earlier in-habitants of the country, and the originators of its civilization and culture; whereas the Semites were invaders who had pressed in from Arabia, or from Northern Mesopotamia (in which case it is still probable that their earlier home was Arabia[1]), and had adopted the Sumerian civilization. However the development of a rich and diversified culture seems to require the inter-mingling of races, the mental quickening which is the product of the fusing of various ideals and mental habits. We may say,

[1] There is considerable reason to suppose that the ancestors of the Semites came into Arabia from North Africa, where they had formed part of a primitive Hamito-Semitic stock. But any such immigration took place, if at all, at such a remote epoch that for practical purposes we here may disregard it. The *Pre-Semite* may have been an African; but the pronounced distinctive characteristics that make up the *Semite* as such were developed in Arabia. (See *BSO. ch. I.*)

therefore, that although its genesis was Sumerian, the civilization of Babylonia, as we find it, was also to a very great degree Semitic. Neither Sumerian alone nor Semite alone could have created it. The ethnic affiliations of the Sumerians are still uncertain, as well as the circumstances under which the Semites entered the land; and investigators are seeking to analyze the complex and intensely interesting civilization produced by the intermingling of these diverse racial elements. At what time these peoples had first come into contact with each other we cannot as yet determine; but it would seem that all memory of the first great clash had vanished, and that the process of fusion had been in operation for a long period, before the opening of history.

The solution of these problems and the correct writing of the history of ancient Babylonia is complicated to a great degree by the character of the material with which we have to deal. Here are, not connected narrative inscriptions, "checked off" by comparison with accurate and fairly complete chronological tables—such as furnish the information upon which the history of Assyria is based—but quantities of more or less isolated records. Votive inscriptions in which a king celebrates a victorious campaign; scraps of royal genealogy; thousands of business documents which furnish valuable suggestions in their dates; some fragmentary lists of dates and remnants of broken king-lists; various inscribed implements and vessels; as well as occasional brief, ambiguous, and often exceedingly unreliable, allusions in the Assyrian and later Babylonian literature—these constitute the sources which we must utilize. Such detached material requires not only translation, but interpretation from the point of view of philology, archaeology, and epigraphy. Naturally there is considerable uncertainty in the reading of evidence so fragmentary and disconnected.

There is much disagreement as to the detailed order of events, and the chronology is still extremely unsettled: in fact estimates with respect to the date of some kings differ by several centuries.

But into the detailed discussion of these matters it is not necessary for us to enter at this time. We shall confine ourselves to a summary, an outline which may be said to represent the consensus of opinion among all parties.

We catch glimpses in the early records of numerous city-states struggling for supremacy—Sumerian warring with Sumerian, and Semite with Semite. The Sumerian Lugalzaggisi, king of Erech and *patesi* of Gishuch, for a while brought the whole of Southern Babylonia into subjection, conducted his armies throughout the adjoining regions, seemingly even to the Mediterranean coast, and proudly called himself "King of the Land." This Sumerian empire fell however in the course of a couple of generations; and the hegemony passed into the hands of the Semitic kings of Kish. These in turn were superseded by the dynasty of Agade, among whom the most famous is Sargon I,[1] whose conquests extended from the Persian Gulf to the Mediterranean and from Arabia to the Mountains of Kurdistan, thus including all Mesopotamia, Elam, and part of Syria. This monarch and his son Naram-Sin claimed the titles "King of Akkad, King of the Four Quarters (of the Universe)." The political dominance of the Semite at this period would appear to be firmly established. The inscriptions are written to a very great extent in Semitic; and the monumental carvings mostly represent bearded Semites, rather than smooth-shaven Sumerians.[2]

However the empire of Agade seems speedily to have disintegrated. The *patesis* of the various cities became practically independent rulers; and Babylonia was once more broken up into a number of city-states. Meanwhile the Sumerian power revived again; and a period of wonderful material prosperity opened in the southern portion of the land. At length, after the lapse of several generations, the Sumerian rulers of Ur first conquered their neighbors in Sumer, and then established their supremacy over Akkad.

[1] *Shar-gani-sharri.*

[2] There is a corresponding distinction in costumes, and in facial profile. (See *HSA. pp. 40–55.*)

The kings of the dynasty thus inaugurated were Ur-Engur, Dungi, Bur-Sin I, Gimil-Sin, and Ibi-Sin. During their reigns the inscriptions are very preponderantly Sumerian, and a like tendency is seen in art and in customs. There are even reasons for suspecting that this Sumerian renaissance was deliberately promoted. Ur-Engur reigned in Ur for eighteen years. He made himself supreme in Southern Babylonia, and conquered a sufficient portion of the North (including in particular the city of Nippur) to call himself "King of Sumer and Akkad." His son Dungi occupied the throne for fifty-eight years. Dungi completed the conquest of Akkad, devastating Babylon and sacking its great temple E-sagila. He also established his authority over Elam. Probably as the result of these conquests, he revived Naram-Sin's title "King of the Four Quarters." Moreover he imitated Sargon and Naram-Sin in claiming for himself divine honors. Temples were erected for his worship; and he anticipated Julius Caesar and Augustus in having a month named for him. He was succeeded by his son Bur-Sin, who was probably already well-advanced in age, and whose reign of nine years was comparatively uneventful. He retained his father's power and likewise was regarded as divine. Both he and his successor were obliged to suppress occasional revolts in the Elamite provinces. Gimil-Sin, son of Bur-Sin, ruled but eight years.[1] He maintained the prowess of the realm, and may even have extended his sway into Syria.[2] But the seeds of decay were already in the kingdom. The highly centralized administration, with its special favoritism for Ur, must have provoked local jealousies. Exaggerated luxury, the result of long-continued prosperity in both peace and war, sapped the Sumerian military spirit. Finally, with a king who was worshipped as one of the gods, and therefore separated by a host of intermediaries from the conduct of

[1] He ruled for only seven entire *calendar* years, which accounts for the length of reign assigned to him in the chronological tables. But his actual reign covered more than eight years. (See *SAD. p. 8.*)

[2] *HSA. p. 300.*

affairs, corruption in many forms must have flourished; which necessarily weakened the loyalty of the people. Ibi-Sin, son of Gimil-Sin, reigned for about a quarter of a century, but over a kingdom whose power was waning. With him the dynasty of Ur came to an end, when the city itself was taken by the Elamites and the last king of Ur-Engur's line was carried away into captivity.[1]

For about two and a quarter centuries the hegemony remained in Sumer with the kings of Isin, although their position was by no means uncontested. At length Elamite invasions and conquests caused a general breaking-up—a return to the early chaotic conditions. This period of confusion, the duration of which is extremely indefinite, closed when Hammurapi of Babylon emerged victorious as the supreme ruler of all Sumer and Akkad; thus securing for Babylon that leadership among the cities of Babylonia which she was never to lose while the Land of Sumer and Akkad retained its name.

(Bibliography on the History: *HSA; HBA. vol. I; EBH; PAAB; KAT. pp. 7–18; TRU; LSG. pp. 1–18; BSO. ch. I.*)

§ 2. THE CHRONOLOGY OF THE DYNASTY OF UR

*The figures in the last column, which, it will be seen, differ very little from those of Myhrmann, follow King's suggestion that Kudur-Nanchundi conquered Ibi-Sin in 2285; and also take account of the fact that Gimil-Sin really reigned more than eight years (see note on p. 4).

King	Entire Yrs. of Reign	*Radau* (1900)	*Jastrow* (1911)	*Myhrmann* (1910)	*
Ur-Engur	18	?	*2300*	*2408–2390*	2403–2385
Dungi	58	*2700*	*2280*	*2390–2332*	2385–2327
Bur-Sin	9	*2650*	*2220*	*2332–2323*	2327–2318
Gimil-Sin	7	*2600*	*2210*	*2323–2316*	2318–2310
Ibi-Sin	25	*2580*	*2200*	*2316–2291*	2310–2285

(Bibliography on the Chronology: *EBH. p. 30; RBBA. p. 430; SAD. pp. 8, 28–33; HSA. pp. 304f.*)

[1] *HSA. p. 304.*

§ 3. THE DREHEM TABLETS

Near the boundary between Akkad and Sumer lay the great city of Nippur. It was reckoned as politically part of Akkad; but its culture seems to have been predominantly Sumerian. Here was located the great temple of the god Enlil. This temple, which bore the exalted name E-kur, "House of the Mountain," was the supreme center of the religious life of all Babylonia throughout the early period. To it both Sumerians and Semites brought their offerings; and it was honored above all other shrines, from the time of the earliest records until it was overthrown by Hammurapi, in pursuance of his policy to make Marduk of Babylon supreme among the gods. Because of this position of religious pre-eminence, being held sacred by all, Nippur seems to have been more or less neutral ground, exempt from the fierce struggles that devastated the rest of the land. So it naturally came to enjoy great material prosperity; and became a place of vast commercial importance. Its site is now called by the Arabs *Niffer*. Here the University of Pennsylvania Expeditions, from 1888 on, have excavated vast quantities of inscribed material, part of which is now in the University of Pennsylvania Museum, and part in the Imperial Museum at Constantinople. Much of this material has been published under the direction of Prof. Hilprecht.

Drehem is the modern name of a small mound, located about three miles south-east of Niffer and a like distance north of the village of Suq el Afej. The University of Pennsylvania Expedition did some tentative excavating here in 1889; but found no indications of anything at all promising. But here, in 1908 or 1909, the Arabs discovered a store of inscribed clay tablets, which they surreptitiously removed, before the Turkish authorities had had opportunity to claim them for the Constantinople Museum. So, during the last four years, these tablets have appeared, in varying quantities, at various places in Europe and America, in the possession of private collectors or in the hands of dealers in Oriental curios.

From these tablets it would appear that, during the latter part of Dungi's reign, the entire period of Bur-Sin and Gimil-Sin, and the first few years of Ibi-Sin, Drehem was the site of the temple market of Nippur. At least here are the archives of a great business administration, the records of various transactions in cattle and grain, lists of offerings, accounts of rent and taxes, and memoranda of miscellaneous matters.

The first notice concerning the Drehem find was given by *Thureau-Dangin* in 1910, in an article in the *Revue d'Assyriologie*, in which he also published thirteen tablets (*RA. VII, pp. 186ff*). In 1911, *H. de Genouillac* produced *La Trouvaille de Drehem*, in which he published 91 tablets from collections in Constantinople and Brussels, and *Tablettes de Drehem*, in which he published and edited 175 tablets from the Musée du Louvre; *S. Langdon* published and edited 68 tablets from the British Museum and the Bodleian Library in *Tablets from the Archives of Drehem;* and *L. Delaporte* published and translated 21 tablets from private collections, in the *Revue d'Assyriologie* (*RA. VIII, 183ff*). The following year, *P. Dhorme* published *Tablettes de Drehem à Jérusalem* (*RA. IX, pp. 39ff*); and *L. Legrain* issued an exceedingly valuable work, *Le Temps des Rois d'Ur*, in which is given the result of the careful study of 390 new tablets which he publishes therewith.

The tablets published in the present book are part of a collection in the hands of the author, and secured for him by Professor Gottheil of Columbia University. The following is a brief description of them.

(Bibliography on Nippur: *PN. II, pp. 245–65; BE. vol. V, Fasciculus I, pp. 26f.*)

(Bibliography on Drehem: *GTD. p. VII; TAD. p. 5; TRU. pp. 5ff; Price* in *AJSL, Apr. 1912, pp. 211ff.*)

§4. DESCRIPTION OF TABLETS

No.	Reign	Date Yr.	Date Mon.	Measure- ments, cm.	Description
I	Dungi	25	2	3.7 x 3.5	Account of 3 gazelles expended
II	"	38	9	3.4 x 3.2	Account of 3 bulls received
III	"	41	7	3.3 x 2.8	Memorandum con- cerning a female slave
IV	"	44	12	3.8 x 3.5	Receipt for timber
V	"	50	11	4.5 x 3.4	Account of sacrifices
VI	"	54	11	2.6 x 2.5	Account of 1 lamb brought in
VII	"	55	1	3.2 x 2.8	Account of clothing
VIII	"	"	10	2.7 x 2.4	Receipt for goats
IX	"	56	12	4. x 3.4	Account of sheep
X	"	"	"	4.1 x 3.1	Account of sacrifices
XI	"	"	5	3.2 x 2.7	Memorandum con- cerning sheep
XII	"	57	11	3.5 x 3.1	Account of sacrifices
XIII	Bur-Sin	2	1	3.2 x 2.8	Receipt for cattle
XIV	"	"	4	4.9 x 3.9	Account concerning tribute in cattle
XV	"	"	5	3.4 x 3.1	Record of tax paid in sheep
XVI	"	"	6	3.6 x 3.	Account of sheep and goats
XVII	"	7	8	5.3 x 3.7	Account of sacrifices
XVIII	"	8	2	4.3 x 4.5	Receipt for tax paid in grain
XIX	"	"	9	4.4 x 3.7	Account of sheep and goats

XX	Bur-Sin	9	2	3.1 x 2.8	Record of payments of palace tribute
XXI	Gimil-Sin	2	8	3.9 x 3.3	Account of sacrifices
XXII	"	3		3.7 x 3.4	Memorandum concerning rent for a ship
XXIII	"	4	1	4. x 3.8	Record of offering for a priestess
XXIV	"	"	11	3.9 x 3.7	Record concerning a bull
XXV	"	5	1	10.7 x 6.7	Inventory of a large herd of cattle
XXVI	"	"	"	4.7 x 4.	Receipt for offerings in grain
XXVII	"	"	10	6. x 4.	Receipt for sheep and goats for various purposes
XVIII	"	7	5	4. x 3.4	Account concerning tribute in lambs
XXIX	"	"	7	4.9 x 4.1	Account of sacrifices
XXX	Ibi-Sin	1	11	4.7 x 3.8	Receipt for cattle

XVIII has faint traces of a seal.

XXIII is broken on the end. Has a seal.

XXIV has a seal, only partly legible, but identical with that on XXIX.

XXV is broken on the edge; but much of what is missing can be supplied.

The date of XXVI and XXVII is made *Gimil-Sin 5* on the basis of *Langdon, TAD. p. 18.*

XXVII has seals, but illegible.

XXIX has a seal.

XXX has a seal.

(Bibliography on the Dates: *ISA. pp. 328ff; SAD. pp. 28ff.*)

9

§ 5. THE LANGUAGE

The language of these tablets is apparently pure Sumerian: that is, except for some few Semitic personal names, there is nothing in them that is distinctively Semitic. Of course it is entirely possible that the use of Sumerian in business documents even at this time was only a conventional survival of ancient custom among a people who already were using the Semitic idiom in ordinary conversation, just as the medical profession of to-day employs a Latin jargon in prescriptions and to some extent in diagnoses. Nay more, these documents may even have been read in Semitic, as we render the Latin abbreviations "*Lb.*" and "*Etc.*," "*pound*" and "*and-so-forth*," without thought of "*librum*" or "*et cetera.*" But this is merely among the possibilities: there is no evidence for it on these tablets. There is not even indication that a single sign was given its Semitic value.

The writing is almost entirely ideographic, and is nearly devoid of definite sentence structure. The text in fact may be said to consist of disconnected notes, in extremely abbreviated form. They remind one in this regard of our present-day invoices, bills of lading, receipts, etc.

Common nouns are generally indicated by a single simple or compound ideogram. (*udu* = sheep; *é* = house; *lugal* = king, etc.) The plural, when indicated, is expressed by doubling of **Grammatical Notes:** the sign (*ni-ni* = gods, XI, O, 3; *sigišše-* **The Noun** *sigišše* = offerings, X, R, 1), or by the termination -*ene* (*kušene* = officers, XXVII, O, 3); but when a numeral is given, no further indication of the plural is deemed necessary. Some nouns have natural gender (*en* = lord; *nin* = lady; *cu-qar* = young she-goat; etc.). In some other cases the feminine is expressed by prefixing *sal* (= female) (*sal-sil* = she-lamb; etc.). Case-inflection generally does not appear; but we find -*e* indicating the *status rectus*, with a force often resembling that of a definite article (*gud-e*, XII, O, 1; *lugal-e*, XIV, R, 8;

10

bir-e, XXVI, R, 6) (see *LSG. pp. 62f*), and *-a* indicating the *status obliquus* (*mal-a*, XVII, R, 4, here it has the force of the genitive) (*LSG. pp. 64ff*). Prefixed *nam-* or *a-* forms abstract nouns (*nam-šid* = priesthood, IX, O, 5; *a-lum* = fruitfulness, XVI, O, 4; *a-sig* = wooliness, VIII, O, 1). Proper nouns are most often written syllabically, "spelled out"; but occasionally employ ideograms. The names of deities and of deified men are regularly preceded by the sign *dingir* (= god). Place-names most frequently have the suffix *-ki* (= place). The determinative *giš* (= wood) precedes wooden articles. (*^{giš}gu-za* = throne, XX, O, 5.)

Adjectives and adjectival expressions generally follow the noun which they qualify (*udu-xul; lugal ligga;* etc.). But there are excep-
The Adjective tions to this rule (*sal-sil;* etc.). Adjectives are ex-
pressed simply and are uninflected. (See *LSG. p.99*.)

The Sumerian language had an elaborate system of prefixes and suffixes, to fulfill the place of both the prepositions and the complete inflexional system of other tongues; and a number of
Prepositions and these prefixes and suffixes appear on these
Prepositional Suffixes tablets. A list follows:

-ge is used to express the genitive, when the genitive so expressed is itself in the status rectus (nominative or accusative) (*lugal uruab^{ki}ma-ge* = king of Ur (subject of sentence), XXV, Col. IV, 8).

-ga is used to express the genitive, when the genitive so expressed is in the status obliquus (*en ^{d}nina uruk^{ki}-ga* = lord of Nina-of-Erech (*^{d}nina uruk^{ki}ga* being itself a genitive related to *en*), XXVI, R, 6).

-ra implies the idea of motion towards, hence may direct the attention to, the word to which it is attached (*še-da-ra*, see note on XVIII, R, 4).

-šu means *towards, unto, up to, until, at,* and even *with* (see *LSG. pp. 70–73*). On these tablets it may generally be translated *for* (*sadug-šu*= for the regular offering, XVIII, O, 2; *^{d}dungi-xegalki-šu* = for Dungi-xegalki, XXII, O, 4; etc.).

11

-*da* implied originally *contact with* (*LSG. p. 73*), *accompaniment,* *intimate relation,* and *purpose* (regarded subjectively) (*LSG. 74-76*) (*še-da* = of the grain, XVIII, O, 2; *é-da* = for a house (intention implied), IV, O, 2; *sag-da* = in chief, XXII, O, 3).

-*ta* means primarily *from;* but, like the Latin *de,* comes to signify *concerning* and may indicate practically a status obliquus or a genitive (see *LSG. pp. 76-78*). (Note the progression: *unâka-ta* = from Unâka, XXII, R, 1; *itu-ta ud XVIII* etc. = when *of* (or *from*) *the month 18 days* etc., V, R, 10; *ša* (= in) *mudura-ta* = in Mudura, XXI, R, 1; *mu éani-ta--šu* = "for the name *of his house,*" XI, O, 2.)

-*ni* is read *in* (see XI, R, 1 and Note, and cf. *Br. 5335* for prepositional use of NI).

Occasionally two suffixes are used together (-*da-ra,* XVIII, R, 4; -*ta-šu,* XI, O, 2). (With reference to this use of double postposition, compare the use of -*ta-ku* in *Macmillan, Religious Texts, No. XXXII* (*BA. V, p. 679*), translated by *Prince* in *JAOS, 1913.*)

There are some elements that, originally nouns, have come when associated with certain suffixes to form a combination with prepositional signification. In such combination the nominal element precedes, while of course the suffix follows, the noun or phrase which the preposition governs. Such combinations are: *ki . . . ta. ki* = *place;* hence *ki*-ABC-*ta* = *from the place of* ABC = *from* ABC (*ki-abbašagga-ta* = from Abbašagga, I, R, 2; etc.)

mu . . . šu. mu = name; hence *mu*-ABC-*ta* = *for the name of* ABC = *intended for,* or *addressed to,* ABC. (*mu-kušene-šu* = intended for the officers, XXVII, O, 3; *mu-nin-šu* = for the lady, XXIII, O, 2; *mu--éani-ta--šu* = intended for his house, XI, O, 2.)

The independent forms of the pronouns (*see LSG. pp. 101ff*) do not appear on these tablets, nor do we find any examples **Pronouns** of the suffixed or infixed forms for the first person. We discover however instances of the attached forms of the second and third persons:

-*zu* (*nita-zu* = *thy* servant, XXIX, S, 8).

-*bi* (*kilal-bi* = *their*, or *its*, value, VII, O, 2 & 4, & R, 1).

-*ba* (*má-II-a-ba-šu* = for *his* two ships, XII, R, 3).

-*ni* (*éa-ni--ta* = for *his* house, XI, O, 2).

-*na* (*sag-da-na* = literally, *its*-in-chief = "*summus*," XXII, O, 3).

-*an*-, infixed direct object (*šu-ba-an-ti* = he has received *them*, XXVII, R, 3; XXX, R, 2).

Here Langdon's theory (see *LSG. pp. 105ff*) of a distinction between animate and inanimate objects seems to break down, nor is the supposed distinction as to the status consistently carried through. In short the various forms of the attached pronoun are yet to be explained.

The verbal forms which appear are few and simple. The abstract idea of the verb, whether infinitive or participial, is expressed by the unaugmented stem (*uš* = stand, *sa* = bind, in *mu uš-sa* = the year which *stands bound* =

The Verb

the year *after;* a very common formula in dates). There is a form consisting of the stem with an over-hanging vowel (or vowel of prolongation) and reduplication of the final consonant, which in usage resembles a passive participle (*zig-ga*, XXVII, O, 6; *temen-na*, XVII, O, 9). The prefix *mu* conveys a definite active idea, while *ba* prefixed indicates a passive, or possibly impersonal, construction. (Compare *mu-xul*, XIV, R, 9, with *ba-xul*, III, R, 4; and *mu-ru*, XXV, Col. IV, 11, with *ba-ru*, XXIV, R, 4.) In the common form *šu-ba-ti*, the stem is *ti* (= take), *šu* gives a strongly active idea (*LSG. p. 144*), and *ba* conveys the thought of one acting from a distance for himself (*LSG. p. 139*); so we translate *he has received* (IV, R, 3; and many other places).

Conjunction

The conjunction *ša* (U) = *and*, appears occasionally; but most often the connective is not expressed.

The numeral 1 appears on these tablets in three forms, a single stroke, either upright, horizontal, or inclined at an angle. The

upright numeral is the one ordinarily employed; but the horizontal form is used before *gur* (a grain-measure = 300 *qa*)
The Numerals (XVIII, O, 1) and the inclined stroke is used in connection with the sign LAL (signifying *loss* or *reduction*, hence = *minus*) (*a-du X-lal-I-kam* = the ninth time, VI, R, 3–4).

2 and 3 employ repetitions of the numeral 1, arranged side-by-side.

4–8 also use repetitions of the 1, but arranged in two rows.

9 is written *X-lal-I* = 10–1 (VI, R, 3).

10 is represented by a corner-wedge.

20 and the other multiples of 10, up to 50, use the proper number of corner-wedges.

Units of lesser denomination are always written after the units of larger denomination (*X.I = XI; XXX.III = XXXIII;* etc.).

60 and multiples of 60 are indicated by the same signs as 1, 2, etc., but generally they are written somewhat larger (*seven-sixties* plus *forty* plus *six = 466*, IV, O, 1). Of course tens follow sixties, as ones follow tens.

600 is represented sometimes by the combination of an upright and a corner-wedge, which combination is repeated for 1200 or other multiples of 600 (*twice-six-hundred* plus *five-sixties = 1500*, XXVI, O, 1). Sometimes it is indicated simply by a large corner-wedge (*twice-six-hundred* plus *twenty* plus *three = 1223*, IV, O, 3).

Naturally there is often uncertainty whether an upright is to be read as a sixty or a unit; and six-hundred is liable to be taken for either seventy or ten.

Fractions employed special signs (*šuššana = ¹/₃*, VII, O, 4).

§ 6.   THE CALENDAR

At the period of these tablets the Calendar was in considerable confusion. Apparently there were several different sets of

onth-names in use in the various cities of the kingdom of Ur.
he following is the system employed at Drehem, which differs
mewhat even from that which was most used in the neigh-
oring city of Nippur.

(1) Aug.–Sept. *itu Mašrukù* = month of eating gazelles
(2) Sept.–Oct. *itu Šešdakù* = month of eating zebu (?) or swine (?)
(3) Oct.–Nov. *itu Une^{xu}kù* = month of eating "*une*-birds"
(4) Nov.–Dec. *itu Kisìg ^dNinasu* = month of the Couch of Ninasu
(5) Dec.–Jan. *itu Ezen ^dNinasu* = month of the Festival of Ninasu
(6) Jan.–Feb. *itu Akiti* = month of the New Year
(7) Feb.–Mar. *itu Ezen ^dDungi* = month of the Festival of Dungi
(8) Mar.–Apr. *itu Šuešša* = ? (probably has some reference to "third month")
(9) Apr.–May *itu Ezen-max* = month of the Great Festival
(10) May–June *itu Ezen Anna* = month of the Festival of Anna
(11) June–July *itu Ezen (^d)Mekigal* = month of the Festival of Mekigal
(11a) (*itu Ezen-dirig-Mekigal*, an intercalary month inserted every four years)
(12) July–Aug. *itu Šeqinkud* = month of the grain-harvest

The months were probably strictly lunar (*TRU. p. 15*); therefore
the frequent introduction of the intercalary month was necessary,
in order to retain the stability of the calendar. The official
year seems to have begun with *Mašrukù* at this time; but the
names *Akiti* and *Šuešša* were apparently remnants of an earlier
system, kept alive by the conservatism of religious ceremonial.

(Bibliography on the Calendar: *EBH. pp. 287–307; TAD.
pp. 6–16; TRU. pp. 13–16*)

§7. PERSONAL NAMES OCCURRING ON TABLETS

Abbašagga. I, II, XIV, XVI, XIX.

Abilzimti (Sem.) = *Bearer-of-Ornament.* XV, XIX.

Adatum. I.

Addakalla. XX.

Axuni (Sem.) = *Our-Brother.* VIII, XI, XVII.

Axupir (Sem.) = *Brother-of-?.* XXV.

Axupiqar (Sem.) = *Brother-of-?.* XII.

Âkalla. I.

dAmar-dEn-zu = iluBur-iliSin q.v.

Anana. VII.

Ašnia. XXX.

Atur. XVII.

Babati. XXVIII.

Barbarnimin(?). IV.

Bidea(?) XIX.

iluBur-iliSin. XIII, XIV, XV, XVI, XX.

Duggašagud. XXVII.

Duggali. XXIX.

dDungi. III. (See also Divine Names.)

dDungi-âmu. XIII, XV.

dDungi-xegalki. XXII.

dDungi-urumu. XXVII.

En-dingir-mu. III, XVII.

En-dDungi. XXIII.

dEnlil-zišaggal. XIX, XXV.

Ennam-dDungi. XXIII.

En-dNina. IX, XIV.

Erimu. XVII, XXVII.

Gimil-iliDungi (or Šu-dDungi) XVII.

iluGimil-iliSin. XXV, XXVIII

Gir-dLux. XV.

Xe-šag(?). XXIII.

Xukuxabma. IX.

Xupiqar-abrabdu(?). XXVII.

Iddâ. XIV.

Idderu. IX.

dIbi-dEnzu = iluIbi-iliSin. XXX.

Idegalurra. X.

Intaéa. XXI, XXVIII.

Ipšaxani (Sem.) = *He-has-pacified-us.* XIV.

Išarbaliggingab. XIV.

Lubalšagga. IX.

Lugal-magurri. XXVIII.

Lugal-nirgal. XI.

Lugal-sidi. III.

Lugal-šešura. XXIX.

Lugal-turra. XVII.

Lukani. XXVI.

Lu-dNingirsu. XXX.

Lu-dNintu. XXX.

Lušagga. IX.

Lušaši. XXX.

Kalakam (Sem.) = *Prince* (?). XIV.

Kalni-ᵈEnzu. XXIII.

Kalux (Sem.) = *Sailor*. XIV.

Iašugazuku. II.

Jalul. XVI.

Karâm-Ilâni (Sem.) = *Beloved-of-the-gods*. XI.

Jekanimur. XVIII.

Jigi. IV.

Jingal. V.

Jinkagina. XVIII.

Jur-ᵈEnzu. XXI, XXVIII.

Jur-ᵈIm. XXVI.

Ciluš-ᵈDagan (Sem.) = *His-Protection-is-Dagan*. IX.

Šepagga. I.

Šešdada. IX.

Šu-ᵈDungi = Gimil-^{ili}Dungi q.v.

ᵈŠu-ᵈEnzu = ^{ilu}Gimil-^{ili}Sin q.v.

Šugaganui. XIV.

Šûdar. XVIII.

Udaralšu. XXVIII.

Unâka. XXII.

Urazagnunna. XXVII.

Ur-ᵈBau, A son of Bur-Sin. XX. (See *EBH. p. 274*.)

Ur-ᵈDungi. XXIX.

Ur-ᵈDungi-sarbimu(?). XXX.

Ur-ᵈGalalim-gišnin(?). XIX.

Ur-ᵈXani. XXIX.

Ur-ᵈLušeka. X.

Urnigingar. VIII, XIII.

Ur-ᵈNingišzidda. XVIII.

Uršugašullu. XXX.

Zubaga. XX.

§ 8. DIVINE NAMES OCCURRING ON TABLETS

Allagula. V.

Anna. VIII; XII; XXVII.

Bau. XX.

Dagan. V; IX.

Dungi (deified king). XIII; XV; XVII; XXII; XXIII; XXVII; XXIX; XXX. (See also Personal Names.)

Enzu. XIII; XIV; XV; XVI; XX; XXI; XXIII; XXV; XXVIII; XXIX; XXX.

Enlil. V; X; XVII; XIX; XXI; XXV; XXIX.

Galalim. XIX.

Im. XXVI.

Xani. XXIX.

Lux. XV.

Lušeka. X.

Mekigal, generally written without the god-sign. V; VI; XII; XXIV; XXX. Occurs on these tablets only in month-name. (See Calendar.)

Nanâ. XII.

Nannar. I; V; XVII; XXI.

Nannar-Qarzida. XX.

Nina (or Innanna). V; IX; X; XII; XIV.

3

Nina (or Innanna) of Erech.
XVII; XXVI; XXVII.
Ninasu. XI; XIV; XV;
XXVIII. Occurs on these
tablets only in month-names.
(See Calendar.)
Ningal(ge). V.
Ningirsu. XXX.

Ningišzidda. XVIII.
Ninlil. V; X; XVII; XX
XXIX.
Nintu. XXX.
Paku. V.
Šig (= ^{ilu}Damqu, *BE, XIV,*
59; BE, XV, p. 54). XII.
Tiladdar. X.

§9. PLACE NAMES OCCURRING ON TABLETS

Adamdun^{ki}, probably located
in Elam (*HSA. p. 290*). IV.
Adluzidaxri^{ki}, unknown. XVII.
Anšan^{ki}, an important province
of Elam; ultimately con-
quered Ur (*HSA. p. 304*). IV.
Enlil^{ki} = Nippur q.v
Erech (Uruk^{ki}), one of the
chief cities of Southern
Babylonia. X, XII, XVII,
XXVI, XXVII.
Eridu (Nun^{ki}), an important
city located on the shore of
the Persian Gulf, at this
time; but now far inland
(*HSA. p. 282*). II, XVIII,
XIX.
Ganxar^{ki}, a district in the
mountains, east of the Tigris
(*HSA. p. 287*). III.
(kalam) Gannagi, unknown.
XII.
Xuxunuri^{ki}, likely in the vicin-
ity of Elam. XVII.
Xumurti^{ki}, probably a district

of Elam (*HSA. p. 287*). IX
XI, XII.
Kimaš^{ki}, located in the vicinit
of Elam (*HSA. p. 290*). IX
X, XI, XII.
Lulubu^{ki}, a principality amon
the Zagros hills (*HSA. p. 55*)
VI.
Luršu^{ki}, unknown. III.
Magan, unknown. VIII.
^{kur}Martu, the western country
(*KAT. pp. 178ff*). IX.
Mudura, unknown XXI.
Nippur (Enlil^{ki}), see Intro-
duction. V, X, XIV.
Nun^{ki} = Eridu q.v.
Pidaltum, unknown. XIII.
Simalum(or -num)^{ki}, probably
an Elamite province. XXII,
XXIII.
Simurum^{ki}, a country prob-
ably in the vicinity of Lulu-
bu and Ganxar (*HSA. p.
287*). VI.

18

Šidtab^{ki}, a city in Northern Babylonia (*HSA. p. 206*). XIV.

Tummal, mentioned frequently on Drehem tablets; but unknown. XVII, XXIX.

Urbilum^{ki}, a province among the Zagros hills (*HSA.p.302*). VII, VIII, XIV, XV, XVI.

Uruk^{ki} = Erech q.v.

Uruab^{ki}ma = Ur, see Introduction. X, XXV, XXVIII, XXIX.

(mada) Zapšali^{ki}, unknown region, conquered by Gimil-Sin. XXVIII, XXIX.

There are excellent maps in HSA and TRU.

§ 10. CLASSIFICATION OF ANIMALS

The following animals are mentioned on these tablets, as used in business transactions, or employed for sacrifice.

gud = ox or bull; also used to indicate the bovine species in general.

gud u(ŠAM) = "ox of (the) meadow" = pastured ox.

gud še = "ox of wheat" = fattened ox (see note on II, 0, 1).

gud mu III = "ox of three years."

gud še šig = fattened ox of fine (first) quality.[1]

gud še šig uš = fattened ox of good (second) quality.[2]

gud še III-kam uš = fattened ox of third quality.

gud še IV-kam uš = fattened ox of fourth quality.

gud amar ga = "ox, young, of milk" = suckling bull-calf.

àb = cow.

àb u = pastured cow.

àb mu II = two-year-old cow.

àb amar ga = suckling cow-calf.

udu = sheep; used also in general to refer to sheep and goats collectively.

udu u = pastured sheep.

---

[1] *šig* = *damiqtu* (*Br. 9446*) = sweet, purified = fine quality.

[2] *šig uš* = "next to fine." Compare Lau's rendering of *uš lugal* (*OBTR.*, p. 39).

udu še = fattened sheep.

udu še šig = fattened sheep of fine quality.

udu še šig uš = fattened sheep of good quality.

udu še III-kam uš = fattened sheep of third quality.

udu še IV-kam uš = fattened sheep of fourth quality.

udu gud-e uš-sa = stall-fed sheep (see note on XII, 0, 1).

udu še gud-e uš-sa = fattened stall-fed sheep.

udu-xul = superior sheep (see note on IX, 0, 1).

udu-xul nigin-ru = superior sheep in perfect condition (see note on IX, 0, 2).

udu a-lum = "fruitful sheep" = pregnant sheep (see note on XVI, 0, 4).

udu a-lum nigin-ru = pregnant sheep in perfect condition.

ganam = ewe.

ganam u = pastured ewe.

ganam še = fattened ewe.

ganam še šig = fattened ewe of fine quality.

ganam-xul = superior ewe.

ganam-xul nigin-ru = superior ewe in perfect condition (XVI, R, 1 ?).

sil = lamb; more particularly, male lamb.

sil še = fattened lamb.

sil gab = "lamb of meal" (fed upon ground grain) = weaned lamb.[1]

sil ga = suckling lamb.

sil udu-xul = lamb of superior sheep.

sal-sil = she-lamb.

sal-sil še = fattened she-lamb.

sal-sil gab = weaned she-lamb.

sal-sil ga = suckling she-lamb.

uz = goat, especially the female (*Br. 3707*).

uz u = pastured goat.

uz a-sig = goat with wool (see note on VIII, 0, 1).

[1] This rendering is based both upon the meaning of *gab* and upon the fact that on Tablet XXV the *sil gab*, *sal-sil gab*, *bir gab*, and *cu-qar gab* are listed between the more mature animals and the sucklings (see XXV, Col. III).

ir-gal[1] = "large kid" = he-goat (*TRU.*, *p. 18*).

ir-gal u = pastured he-goat.

ir-gal še = fattened he-goat.

ir-gal še šig = fattened he-goat of fine quality.

ir-gal še šig uš = fattened he-goat of good quality.

ir-gal še III-kam uš = fattened he-goat of third quality.

ir-gal še IV-kam uš = fattened he-goat of fourth quality.

ir-gal še gud-e uš-sa = fattened stall-fed he-goat.

ir[2] = kid; more particularly, male kid.

bir še = fattened kid.

bir gab = weaned kid.

bir ga a-sig = suckling kid with wool.

cu-qar[3] = young she-goat, goat-heifer.

cu-qar še = fattened goat-heifer.

cu-qar še šig = fattened goat-heifer of fine quality.

cu-qar še šig uš = fattened goat-heifer of good quality.

cu-qar še III-kam uš = fattened goat-heifer of third quality.

cu-qar še IV-kam uš = fattened goat-heifer of fourth quality.

cu-qar gab = weaned she-kid.

cu-qar ga = suckling she-kid.

cu-qar ga ud = suckling she-kid, a day old (see note on XIII, 0, 1).

anšu še = fattened ass.

maš-ru = gazelle.

amar maš-ru = young gazelle.

siqqa-bar še = fattened antelope.

---

[1] Read *máš-gal* by some of the best and most recent authorities.

[2] Also read *máš*.

[3] Also read *sal-áš-qar*.

PART II

TEXT OF THE TABLETS

I

1) I amar maš-ru(KAK)
   1 *young gazelle*
2) e(BIT) še-pag(XU)-ga
   (for the) house (of) Šepagga
3) a-a-kal-la pa-kabar
   Âkalla (being the) " great official "
4) II amar maš-ru(KAK) ba-til(BE)
   2 *young gazelles, slaughtered,*
5) e(BIT)-dub-ba--šu(KU)
   for (the) record-house
6) mu-gub a-da-tum
   on hand (in charge of) Adatum

1) ud II-kam
   (on the) second day
2) ki--ab-ba-šag-ga--ta ba-zig
   expended by Abbašagga
3) itu šeš-da-kù
   (in the) month (of) Šešdaku
4) mu en ᵈuru-ki ba-tug(KU)
   (in the) year (when the) high-priest (of) Nannar was installed

III

3 *(young gazelles)*

Obv. 5: *e-dub-ba* = house of tablets

22

ev. 2: Abbašagga. This name is of very frequent occurrence
the Drehem inscriptions, and is found on five tablets in this
ollection.

en(= lord) used thus seems best rendered High Priest.

dge: A numeral placed thus on the edge generally represents
e total.

II

OBVERSE

) X gud še
  10 *fattened bulls*

) II gud
  2 *bulls*

) ud XXI-kam
  (*on the*) *twenty-first day*

) ki--ab-ba-šag-ga--ta
  from Abbašagga

) ma-šu-ga-zu-ku
  Mašugazuku (*being*)

REVERSE

1) ni-ku
   shepherd

2) itu ezen max
   (*in the*) *month* (*of the*) *Great Festival*

3) mu en nun^{ki} ba-tug(KU)
   (*in the*) *year* (*when the*) *high-priest* (*of*) *Eridu was installed*

EDGE

XII
12 (*bulls*)

Obv. 1: *gud* *še* = " bull (or ox) of wheat." Compare the
English term " corn-fed."

III

OBVERSE

1) I(?) geme
   1 *female slave*
2) lu-ur-šu^{ki}
   (*in*) *Luršu*
3) ša-šu uš-sa lugal
   property belonging to (*the*) *king*
4) mu-gub
   on hand
5) ki--lugal-si-di--ta
   from Lugalsidi
6) en-dingir-mu
   Endingirmu (*being in charge*)

REVERSE

1) itu ezen ^ddun-gi-
   (*when*) *of the month* (*of the*) *festival* (*of*) *Dungi*
2) -ta ud VII ba-ra-ni
   7 days were come
3) mu a-du II-kam
   (*in the*) *year* (*when for the*) *second time*
4) gan-xar^{ki} ba-xul
   Ganxar was laid waste

Obv. 1: The numeral here is indistinct; it may possibly be X.
3: UŠ = *emêdu* = to stand. Sa = *rakasu* = to bind. " Standing bound " = belonging to, etc.
Rev. 2: *ra* = DU, common word for motion; here = arrive,
come. *Ni* is probably the suffix of 3p. pl. *cp. MSL. p. 257.*

IV

OBVERSE

1) CDLXVI giš eme ša(GAR)
   466 (*logs of*) "*tongue-wood*," *trimmed*

24

CCXVI giš e(BIT)-da
216 (*timbers of*) *wood for house(s)*
MCCXXIII giš ur
1223 *beams*
giš a-dam-dunki
(*it is*) *wood* (*from*) *Adamdun*
mu-gub
on hand

REVERSE

gir ni-gi
(*the*) *overseer* (*being*) *Nigi*
bar(MAŠ)-bar(MAŠ)-ni-min
Barbarnimin(?)
šu-ba-ti
has received
itu še-qin-kud
(*in the*) *month* (*of*) *Šeqinkud*
mu an-ša-anki ba-xul
(*in the*) *year* (*when*) *Anšan was laid waste*

Obv. 1: "Tongue-wood," Lau's reading. ŠA or GAR = to cut
etc.
2: *da*, prepositional suffix.
3: *giš ur* = literally " wood of enclosure."
1, 2, & 3: See Part I, § 5, Numerals.

OBVERSE

V

1) I udu še II sil
    1 *fattened sheep* (*and*) 2 *lambs*
2) dnin-lil
    (*for*) *Ninlil*
3) I udu še II sil
    1 *fattened sheep* (*and*) 2 *lambs*

4) ᵈen-lil
   (*for*) *Enlil*
5) I ganam ᵈnin-gal(MAL)-ge
   1 *ewe* (*for*) *Ningal(ge)*
6) I udu šam(U)
   1 *pastured sheep*
7) ᵈal-la-gu-la
   (*for*) *Allagula*
8) a(ID) ud temen-na kam
   (*the*) *day's allowance was brought in*
9) I udu še I sil
   1 *fattened sheep* (*and*) 1 *lamb*

REVERSE

1) ᵈnin-lil
   (*for*) *Ninlil*
2) I bir ᵈen-lil
   1 *kid* (*for*) *Enlil*
3) I udu še ᵈuru-ki
   1 *fattened sheep* (*for*) *Nannar*
4) I ganam še ᵈnina
   1 *fattened ewe* (*for*) *Nina*
5) I udu še ᵈnin-lil
   1 *fattened sheep* (*for*) *Ninlil*
6) I udu še ᵈpa-ku
   1 *fattened sheep* (*for*) *Paku*
7) a(ID) duk zig-ga
   (*the*) *portion* (*for the*) *pot was expended*
8) er(A-ŠI) sigišše-sigišše ša(LIB) en-lilᵏⁱ
   penitential offerings in Nippur
9) gir nin-gal(MAL)
   (*the*) *overseer* (*being*) *Ningal*
10) itu--ta ud XVIII ba-ra-ni
    (*when*) 18 *days of* (*the*) *month were come*
11) zig-ga a(ID) bil-ni-a
    expended was (*the*) *portion for* (*the*) *fire*

26

2) itu ezen me-ki-gal(IK)
  (*in the*) *month* (*of the*) *festival* (*of*) *Mekigal*

mu uš-sa e(BIT)-kù ša-iši-ᵈda-gan ba-ru
(*in the*) *year after* (*the*) *refectory Ša-iši-Dagan was built*

bv. 5: *ningalge.* -*ge* is the genitive suffix, attached here as a
eminiscence of the etymological derivation of the name Ningal,
. Lady-of-the-Palace.

  ud temenna. This rendering is on Lau's authority (*OBTR.*
ign-List, p. 11).

  : *kam.* *k*- is probably the same element as in the genitive
uffix -*ka*, plus *am*(= is).   (See *LSG. p. 88.*)

tev. 7: This certainly refers to the portion of a sacrifice which
vas cooked and eaten.

: *er.* The signs A-ŠI signify " water of the eye " = a tear.
Ience the reading " tear-offerings " = penitential offerings.

0: See Note on III, R, 1–2.

1: The reference evidently is to the burnt offering.

Edge: This is the date which Radau(*EBH. p. 262*) and Lau
(*OBTR. p. 4*) render,--*mu uš-sa* e(BIT) *ip*(IBIRA) *ša iši-*ᵈ*da-gan*
a-ru,--and translate,--" the year after the *damqar* of Iši-Dagan
built a house (for Dungi?)."   But the fifth sign is clearly KÙ,
not IP; and *ba-ru* is a passive form (see Part I, § 5, The Verb)
e-kù = house of eating (See *OBTR. Sign-List, p. 31*).

VI

1) I sil
    1 *lamb*
2) te-te
    brought in
3) mu-gub
    on hand

4) itu ezen me-ki-gal
   (in the) month (of the) festival (of) Mekigal

1) mu si-mu-ru-um-
   (in the) year (when) Simurum
2) -ᵏⁱ ša(U) lu-lu-bu-
   and Lulubu
3) -ᵏⁱ a-du IX-kam
   (the) ninth time
4) ba-xul
   were laid waste

ud XVII-kam
(on the) seventeenth day

Obv. 2: TE-TE = *qapu* = deliver, etc.   (*SAI, 5705.*)
Rev. 3: See Part I, § 5, Numerals.

VII

1) VIII ku lum-za du(GIN)
   8 fine(?) garments there were(?)
2) ki-lal-bi XXXIII ma-na
   their value (was) 33 minas
3) V ku uš-bar
   5 woven garments
4) ki-lal-bi XIII šuššana ma-na
   their value 13 1/3 minas
5) I ku muqqu
   1 inferior garment

1) ki-lal-bi III ma-na X gin(TU)
   its value 3 minas (and) 10 shekels

28

ki--a(ID)-na-na--ta
from Anana
mu-gub
on hand
itu maš-ru-kú
(in the) month (of) Mašruku
mu ur-bi-lum^ki ba-xul
(in the) year (when) Urbilum was laid waste

bv. 1: *lum-za* = plenty-of-jewels. DU = *mîn* = to be
 Literally " garments of the weaver."

VIII

OBVERSE

I uz a-sig
1 *goat with wool*
I bir ga a-sig
1 *suckling kid with wool*
I cu-qar ga má-gan
1 *suckling she-kid (of) Magan*
ba-til(BE)
slaughtered;
ud VIII-kam
(on the) eighth day

REVERSE

ki--a-xu-ni--ta
from Axuni
ur-nigin-gar
Urnigingar
šu-ba-ti
has received
itu ezen an-na
(in the) month (of the) festival (of) Anna
mu ur-bi-lum-
(in the) year (when) Urbilum

6) -^{ki} ba-xul
    was laid waste

Obv. 1: *uz* or *gaz* is undoubtedly a Semitic loan-word: com
pare Assyrian *enzu*, Hebrew עֵז, Arabic *'anzu^n*
a- is an abstract prefix. So *uz a-sig* = literally, " goat (
woolliness."

IX

OBVERSE

1) CLXV udu-xul
    145 *sheep of fine quality*
2) XIII udu-xul nigin-ru(KAK)
    13 *sheep of fine quality, in perfect condition*
3) CXX bir-gal
    120 *he goats*
4) LX sil udu-xul
    60 *lambs (of) sheep of fine quality*
5) nam-šid-ak ^{kur}mar-tu
    (*at the*) *establishment of* (*the*) *western priesthood*
6) gir xu-uku-xa-ab-ma
    (*the*) *overseer* (*being*) *Xukuxabma*
7) LX sil ci-lu-uš-^{d}da-gan
    60 *lambs (of) Ciluš-Dagan*

REVERSE

1) CXX sil en-^{d}nina
    120 *lambs (of) En-Nina*
2) CXX sil šeš-da-da šid
    120 *lambs (of) Šešdada* (*the*) *priest*
3) LX sil lu-pal-šag-ga
    60 *lambs (of) Lupalšagga*
4) LX sil lu-šag-ga
    60 *lambs (of) Lušagga*

5) LX amar maš-ru(KAK) id-de-ru
   60 *young gazelles (of) Idderu*
6) mu-gub itu še-qin-kud
   on hand (in the) month (of) Šeqinkud
7) mu ki-maš(BAR)ᵏⁱ ša(U) xu-mur-tiᵏⁱ ba-xul
   (in the) year (when) Kimaš and Xumurti were laid waste

EDGE

ud VII-kam
(on the) seventh day

Obv. 1: *udu-xul. xul* = Ass. *xidûtu* = joy, etc. This phrase naturally suggests our own idea, *de luxe*, i. e. fine quality.

2: *nigin-ru. nigin*(GURUN) = primarily *enclosure*—hence, *fullness, plenty*, etc. (*MSL. pp. 168, 258, etc.*) *ru*(KAK) = *build, make, produce*, etc. (*MSL. p. 277, etc.*) The combination seems to mean 'making complete.'

5: *nam*, an abstract prefix. *šid* = priest. Hence *nam-šid* = priesthood. *ak* = make, establish, etc. ᵏᵘʳ*martu* seems at this time to refer in a general way to the western lands. Later it denotes more specifically Palestine (*see Vanderburgh, in JBL. 1913.*)

X

OBVERSE

1) I sil
   1 *lamb*
2) ᵈnina
   (for) Nina
3) I sil ᵈnin-lil
   1 *lamb (for) Nin-lil*
4) I sil ᵈen-lil
   1 *lamb (for) En-lil*
5) a-du I-kam
   (the) first time
6) I sil ᵈnina
   1 *lamb (for) Nina*

7) I sil ᵈnin-lil
   1 *lamb (for) Nin-lil*
8) a-du II-kam
   (*the) second time*

REVERSE

1) I udu še sigišše-sigišše ᵈnina
   1 *fattened sheep, offerings (for) Nina*
2) a-du III-kam
   (*the) third time*
3) ša(LIB) en-lilᵏⁱ
   in Nippur
4) I ganam II cu-qar
   1 *ewe (and) 2 goat-heifers*
5) sigišše-sigišše ud-sar ša(LIB) urugᵏⁱ-ga
   offerings (at the) new moon in Erech
6) IV cu-qar e(BIT) ᵈtil-la-ad-dar nir
   4 *goat-heifers (for the) house (of) Tilladdar (the) prince*
7) xar ᵈtil-la-ad-dar-ra ba-an-ku
   (*when the) decree (of) Tilladdar commanded it*
8) ša(LIB) uru-abᵏⁱ-ma
   in Ur
9) gir i-de-gal-ur-ra
   (*the) overseer (being) Idegalurra*
10) itu--ta ud XXX-ba-ra-ni
    (*when) of (the) month 30 days were come*
11) zig-ga ur-ᵈlu-še-ka(DUG)
    expended (by) Ur-Lušeka
12) itu še-qin-kud
    (*in the) month (of) Šeqinkud*

EDGE

mu ki-maš(BAR)ᵏⁱ ba-xul
(*in the) year (when) Kimaš was laid waste*

Obv. 5 & 8, & Rev. 2: The references to " first time," " second time," etc. on this tablet apparently have to do with successive offerings.

Rev. 10: See Note on IV, R, 2.

XI

OBVERSE

1) IV udu
   4 *sheep*
2) mu--e-a-ni--ta-šu(KU)
   for his house
3) na-ra-am-NI-NI pa-kabar(RIM)
   Naram-ilâni (being the) great-official
4) ki--a-xu-ni--ta
   from Axuni
5) lugal-ner-gal sukkal ni-ku
   Lugal-nergal (being) messenger-shepherd

REVERSE

1) itu ud XVIII-ba-ni
   (on the) eighteenth day of (the) month
2) itu ezen ᵈnin-a-su
   (in the) month (of the) festival (of) Ninasu
3) mu ki-maš(BAR)ᵏⁱ ša(U)
   (in the) year (when) Kimaš and
4) xu-mur-tiᵏⁱ ba-xul
   Xumurti were laid waste

Obv. 2: *mu* ..... *šu.* *mu* = *šumu* = name. Hence this line = literally, " for the name of his house " = " intended for his house."

ta-šu, double preposition.

3: NI-NI = plural of *dingir*. Hence *naram-ilâni* (" Beloved-of-the-gods "), a purely Semitic name, seems the correct reading here.

Rev. 1: Literally "month day XVIII-its-in." (See *Br. 5335*.)

4   33

XII

OBVERSE

1) I udu gud-e uš-sa
   1 *stall-fed sheep*
2) gi-ra-lum ᵈnina
   slaughtered (as an) entire (offering for) Nina
3) I gud še III udu še
   1 *fattened ox (and)* 3 *fattened sheep*
4) ᵈnina
   (for) Nina
5) I udu še
   1 *fattened sheep*
6) ᵈna-na-a
   (for) Nanâ
7) I udu gud-e uš-sa
   1 *stall-fed sheep*

REVERSE

1) e(BIT)-kal ᵈšig
   (for the) temple (of) Šig
2) II udu u(ŠAM)
   2 *pastured sheep*
3) id má II-a-ba--šu(KU)
   allowance for his two ships
4) zig-ga má an-na
   expended (for the) ship (of) Anna
5) ša(LIB) uru(k)ᵏⁱ-ga
   in Erech
6) ki--kalam(UN)--gan-na-gi--ta
   from (the) people (of) Gannagi
7) gir a-xu-pi-qar
   (the) overseer (being) Axupiqar
8) itu ezen me-ki-gal ud XXV-ba-ra-ni
   (when) 25 *days (of the) month (of the) festival (of) Mekigal were
   come*

34

9) mu uš-sa ki-maš^{ki} ša(U) [Xu]mur-ti^{ki} ba-xul
   (*in the*) *year after Kimaš and [Xu]murti were laid waste*

Obv. 1: *gud-e uš-sa:*—Literally, "the cattle (*gud-e*), standing
(*uš*), bound (*sa*)." Evidently these were stall-fed sheep.
2: *gi-ra = dâku (SAI. 1614)* = slaughter. *lum* = plenteousness.
3: These "ships" are the sacred arks used in the religious
ceremonies, similar to the ancient Egyptian sacred boats.
Rev. 4: The dingir(AN)-sign is regularly omitted before the name
Anna, to avoid repetition of the AN.
7: *A-xu-pi-qar.* The third syllable in this name is secured by
comparison with other tablets.
8: See Note on IV, R, 2.

XIII

OBVERSE

1) I cu-qar ga ud
   1 *suckling she-kid* (*a*) *day* (*old*)
2) ša(LIB) pi-dal-tum
   in Pidaltum
3) I àb
   1 *cow*
4) V udu
   5 *sheep*
5) I ?--?
   1 *? ?*
6) I uz
   1 *goat*
7) V sil
   5 *lambs*
8) I sal-sil
   1 *she-lamb*

1) I sil ga
   1 *suckling lamb*

2) I sal-sil ga
   1 *suckling she-lamb*

3) ba-til(BE) ud IV-kam
   slaughtered; (on the) fourth day

4) ki--ᵈdun-gi-a-a-mu--ta
   from Dungi-âmu

5) ur-nigin-gar
   Urnigingar

6) šu-ba-ti
   has received

7) itu maš-ru-kù
   (in the) month (of) Mašruku

8) mu uš-sa ᵈamar-ᵈen-zu lugal
   (in the) year after (the) divine Bur-Sin (became) king

Obv. 1: This line runs literally: " 1 young-she-goat(cu-qar) (of) milk (of a) day."
5: Very indistinct.

XIV

1) I sil en-ᵈnina
   1 *lamb (of) En-Nina*

2) IV udu I bir
   4 *sheep, 1 kid*

3) ip-ša-xa-ni lu-kabar(RIM)
   (of) Ipšaxani (the) high official

4) II sil pa-te-si en-lilᵏⁱ
   2 *lambs (of the) governor (of) Nippur*

5) I sil id-da-a
   1 *lamb (of) Iddâ*

6) I sil i-šar-ba-lig(KAL)-gin(DU)-gab(a)
   1 *lamb (of) Išarbaliggingab*

36

7) I sil .pa-te-si šid-tab^{ki}
   1 *lamb (of the) governor (of) Šidtab*

8) I sil šu-ga-ga-nu-i?
   1 *lamb (of) Šugaganui(?)*

REVERSE

1) I sil ma-lux qa-šu-gab
   1 *lamb (of) Malux (the) grain-measurer*

2) IV udu še I sil mal(GAL)-gi
   4 *fattened sheep, (and) 1 lamb (of) Malgi*

3) ud XXIII-kam
   (*on the*) *twenty-third day*

4) mu-gub lugal
   on hand, royal property,

5) ab-ba-šag-ga ni-ku
   Abbašagga (being) shepherd

6) itu ki-sìg ^dnin-a-su
   (*in the*) *month (of) Kisig Ninasu*

7) mu ^damar-^den-zu
   (*in the*) *year (when the) divine Bur-Sin,*

8) lugal-e ur-bi-lum^{ki}
   the king, (the city of) Urbilum

9) mu-xul
   laid waste

EDGE

XVIII
18 (*sheep, etc.*)

Obv. 3: ip-ša-xa-ni might also be read " (The) ibira Šaxani,"
etc.
Rev. 1: qa-šu-gab = literally, the one whose hand(ŠU) presents
(GAB) the measure(QA).
Rev. 4–5: Another possible rendering for these lines is: " On
hand; Lugal-abbašagga being shepherd."   See XXVIII. O, 4–6.
Rev. 8: Lugal-e, *status rectus*.   See *LSG. pp. 62 ff.*

XV

OBVERSE

1) XXX udu še
   30 *fattened sheep*
2) sa-dug a-bil(NE)-zi-im-ti
   (the) regular offering (of) Abilzimti
3) itu I-kam
   (on the) first (day of the) month
4) gir-ᵈlux pa-kabar
   Gir-Lux (being the) " great official "

REVERSE

1) ki--ᵈdun-gi-a-a-mu--ta
   by Dungi-âmu
2) ba-zig
   were delivered
3) itu ezen ᵈnin-a-su
   (in the) month (of the) festival (of) Ninasu
4) mu ᵈamar- ᵈen-zu
   (in the) year (when the) divine Bur-Sin,
5) lugal-e ur-bi-
   the king, Urbi-
6) lumᵏⁱ mu-xul
   lum laid waste

EDGE

XXX
30 *(sheep)*

Obv. 2: Abilzimti, a purely Semitic name.
Rev. 5: See Note on XII, R, 8.

XVI

OBVERSE

1) I sil še
   1 *fattened lamb*

2) II cu-qar še
   2 *fattened goat-heifers*
3) I udu
   1 *sheep*
4) VII udu a-lum
   7 *pregnant sheep*
5) III udu a-lum nigin-ru(KAK)
   3 *pregnant sheep, in perfect condition(?)*
6) X udu-xul II udu-xul nigin-ru(KAK)
   10 *sheep of fine quality, (and) 2 sheep of fine quality, in perfect condition(?)*

REVERSE

1) II ganam-xul I ganam-xul (nigin-ru?)
   2 *ewes of fine quality, (and) 1 ewe of fine quality (in perfect condition?)*
2) [III] bir
   [3] *kids*
3) ud XXIII-kam
   (*on the*) *twenty-third day*
4) ki--ab-ba-šag-ga--ta
   from Abbašagga
5) na-lul ni-ku
   Nalul (being the) shepherd
6) itu à-ki-ti
   (*in the*) *month (of) Akiti*
7) mu ᵈamar-ᵈen-zu lugal
   (*in the*) *year (when the) divine Bur-Sin, (the) king,*
8) ur-bi-lumᵏⁱ
   Urbilum
9) mu-xul
   laid waste

EDGE

XXXII
32 (*sheep, etc.*)

Obv. 4: *a-lum* = fruitfulness. A; prefix denoting the abstract

39

idea; LUM signifying fruit, plenty, etc. So *udu alum* = fruitful sheep.

5 & 6: *nigin-ru*, See Note on XV, O, 2.

XVII

OBVERSE

1) I udu še
    1 *fattened sheep*
2) ᵈen-lil ᵈnin-lil
    (for) Enlil (and) Ninlil
3) I udu še ᵈuru-ki
    1 *fattened sheep (for) Nannar*
4) a(ID) gig(MI) ba-a
    (a) night's allowance given
5) lugal-tur-ra
    (by) Lugalturra
6) III udu še I bir-gal še
    3 *fattened sheep (and)* 1 *fattened he-goat*
7) ᵈen-lil ᵈnin-lil
    (for) Enlil (and) Ninlil
8) I bir-gal še ᵈuru-ki
    1 *fattened he-goat (for) Nannar*
9) a(ID) ud temen-na
    (a) day's allowance brought in
10) gir a-tur qa-šu-gab
    (the) overseer (being) Atur (the) grain-measurer
11) II udu še
    2 *fattened sheep*

REVERSE

1) ᵈnina uruk^{ki}--šu
    (for) Nina (of) Erech
2) gir a-xu-ni qa-šu-gab
    (the) overseer (being) Axuni (the) grain-measurer
3) I udu še I bir-gal
    1 *fattened sheep (and)* 1 *he-goat*

4) dun-mal-a ad-lu-zi-da-ax-ri^{ki}

(for the) steward (of) Adluzidaxri

5) gir šu-^ddun-gi-(?)

(the) overseer (being) Gimil-Dungi(?--?)

6) eri-mu pa-kabar

Erimu (being the) great official

7) itu ud II-ba-ni

(on the) second day (of the) month

8) ša(LIB) tum-ma-al

in Tummal

9) ki--en-dingir-mu--ta

by Endingirmu

10) ba-zig

was expended

11) itu šu-eš-ša

(in the) month (of) Šuešša

12) mu xu-uxu-nu-ri^{ki} ba-xul

(in the) year (when) Xuxunuri was laid waste

EDGE

XI

11 *(sheep, etc.)*

Obv. 4: *ba-a* = *qašu* = present, give, etc.

9: This rendering is on Lau's authority. (See *OBTR. Sign-List, p. 11.*)

10: *qa-šu-gab.* See Note on XIV, R, 1.

Rev. 4: *dun* = great one, leader, etc. (*MSL. p. 90*) *mal*(GAL) = house. Hence the reading " steward "—compare *major domus.*

7: See Note on XI, R, 1.

XVIII

OBVERSE

1) I. CXX še. gur. lugal

1 gur (and) 120 (qa) finest wheat

2) sa-dug(KA)--šu(KU)

for (the) regular offering

41

3) ki--šu-u-dar--ta
   from Šûdar
4) ne-ka-ni-mùr
   Nekanimur

REVERSE

1) šu-ba-ti
   has received
2) dub nin-ka-gi-na
   (per) tablet (of) Ninkagina
3) ib-ra
   (the) ibra
4) še-da-ra dub-ba
   of (the) wheat, delivery was made
5) gir ur-ᵈnin-giš-zid-da ma-du-du
   (the) overseer (being) Ur-Ningišzidda (the) skipper
6) itu šeš-da-kù
   (in the) month (of) Šešdaku
7) mu en nunᵏⁱ ba-tug(KU)
   (in the) year (when the) high-priest (of) Eridu was installed

Obv. 1: The first numeral is read with the GUR at the end of the line, while the second numeral is read with QA understood before ŠE. When a numeral occurs before ŠE(= wheat), the measure is often omitted—just as in bills etc. to-day "3 1/2 sugar" is naturally taken as referring to "pounds." (See Pɛrt I, § 5, Numerals.)

Rev. 4: *šedara. da-ra,* double postposition. Literally, "as to the wheat, of it (ie, the wheat) was delivery made." *dub-ba,* vb. *dub* with phonetic complement.

XIX

OBVERSE

1) X gud še
   10 fattened oxen
2) XVI udu še
   16 fattened sheep

42

3) IV udu še gud-e uš-sa
   4 *fattened sheep, stalled cattle*
4) X bir gal še
   10 *fattened he-goats*
5) LXX udu
   70 *sheep*
6) XX bir gal
   20 *he-goats*
7) bi(GAŠ)-de-a
   (*in charge of*) *Bidea*

REVERSE

1) gir ᵈen-lil-zi-šag-gal
   (*the*) *overseer* (*being*) *Enlil-zišaggal*
2) mu-gub a-bil-zi-im-ti
   on hand (*for*) *Abilzimti*
3) ki--ur-ᵈgal-alim-giš-nin--ta
   from Ur-Galalim-gišnin
4) ud IX-kam
   (*on the*) *ninth day*
5) mu-gub
   on hand
6) ab-ba-šag-ga ni-ku
   Abbašagga (*being*) *shepherd*
7) itu ezen max
   (*in the*) *month* (*of the*) *Great Festival*
8) mu en nunᵏⁱ ba-tug(KU)
   (*in the*) *year* (*when the*) *lord* (*of*) *Eridu was installed*

EDGE

CXXX
130 (*cattle*)

Obv. 3: See Note on XXVIII, O, 1.
Rev. 2: The name here is very indistinct; but is read by comparison with XVII, O, 2.
Rev. 4: See Part I, §5, Numerals.

XX

OBVERSE

1) II udu še
   2 *fattened sheep*

2) a-du I-kam
   (the) first time;

3) I udu še a-du II-kam
   1 *fattened sheep, (the) second time;*

4) I udu še a-du III-kam
   1 *fattened sheep, (the) third time;*

5) ^{giš}gu-za ^damar-^den-zu
   (for the) throne (of the) divine Bur-Sin

6) ur-^dba-u mu-pa-kabar(RIM)
   Ur-Bau (being) " great official " (for the) year

REVERSE

1) itu ud IX-ba-ni
   (on the) ninth day of the month

2) ki--zu-ba-ga--ta
   from Zubaga

3) ba-zig
   (they) were expended

4) gir ad-da-kal-la dub-sar
   (the) overseer (being) Addakalla (the) scribe

5) itu šeš-da-kù
   (in the) month (of) Šešdaku

6) mu en ^duru-ki-
   (in the) year (when the) high priest (of) Nannar-

7) qar-zi-da ba-tug(KU)
   -Qarzida was installed

EDGE

IV udu
(total) 4 sheep

Obv. 2: See Note on XIII.
5: Probably palace tribute.

44

6: This Ur-Bau was a son of Bur-Sin *(EBH. p. 274)*
Rev. 1: See Part I, § 5, Numerals.

XXI

OBVERSE

1) I gud še III-kam uš
   1 *fattened ox, third quality*
2) II udu še šig uš
   2 *fattened sheep, good quality*
3) II udu-xul II sil
   2 *superior sheep (and) 2 lambs*
4) ᵈen-lil ᵈnin-lil
   (for) Enlil (and) Ninlil
5) I sil ᵈuru-ki
   1 *lamb (for) Nannar*
6) I sil ᵈnin-lil
   1 *lamb (for) Ninlil*
7) ᵈen-lil-zi-ša(g)-gal(IK) pa-kabar
   Enlil-zišagal (being the) " great official "

REVERSE

1) ša(LIB)--mu-du-ra--ta
   in Mudura
2) ud X-kam
   (on the) tenth day
3) ki--in-ta-e(UD-DU)-a--ta
   by Intaea
4) ba-zig
   were expended
5) gir nu-ur-ᵈen-zu dub-sar
   (the) overseer (being) Nur-Enzu (the) scribe
6) itu šu-eš-ša
   (in the) month (of) Šuešša

7) mu ma dara-zu-ab ba-ab-gab
(in the) year (when the) ship Dara-zuab (= Antelope-of-the-Deep) was launched

EDGE

I gud VIII udu
(Total) 1 ox (and) 8 sheep

Obv. 2: šig = *damiqtu* = sweet, purified
3: udu-xul: See Note on X, O, 1.
Rev. 1: ša .... ta: Prefix and suffix.   See Part I, § 5, Prepositions etc.

XXII

OBVERSE

1) I. CCXL še.gur
1 *gur (and)* 240 *(qa of) wheat*
2) id(A) ma--šu(KU) mal
it is rent for (a) ship
3) sag-da-na TA-RA(?)
(the) entire sum ? . . . ?
4) ᵈdun-gi-xe-gal-ki--šu
for Dungi-xegalki
5) pa-al u(ŠA)-a
(the) elderly seer

REVERSE

1) u(ŠA)-na-a-ka--ta
from Unâka
2) mu si-ma-lumᵏⁱ ba-xul
(in the) year (when) Simalum was laid waste

Obv. 1: See Note on XVIII I. O. I.
2: ID(A) = allowance, portion, rent, etc.   MÀ = ship.   MAL = *existence*, hence = " *is.*"

SAG = head, chief, etc. DA = in. NA = its. (See Part
  I, § 5, Pronouns.)

XXIII

OBVERSE

I cu-qar še
1 *fattened goat-heifer*
mu--nin--šu
for (the) lady
ki--mal-ni-^den-zu--ta
from Malni-Enzu(Sin)
en-nam-^ddun-gi
Ennam-Dungi (being the)
[ni]-ku
shepherd

REVERSE

[ud] V-kam
(on the) fifth [day]
itu maš-ru-kù
(in the) month (of) Mašruku
mu uš-sa si-ma-
(in the) year after Sima-
-lum^{ki} ba-xul
-lum was laid waste

SEAL

1) ^dšu-^den-zu
     divine Gimil-Sin
2) lugal lig(KAL)-ga
     mighty king
3) lugal uru-ab^{ki}-ma
     king of Ur
4) lugal an-ub-da tab-tab-ba
     king of (the) Four Regions

5) en-^d
   En-
6) -dun-gi
   -Dungi
7) [dup-sar?]
   [*(the) scribe*]
8) du xe(GAN)-šag
   son (of) Xešag
9) nita
   (the) servant

Obv. 2: *nin* (= lady) must here refer to a priestess.

XXIV

OBVERSE

1) I gud še šig
   1 *fattened bull of fine quality,*
2) ba-dug(KA)
   promised
3) mu-gub xum--šu
   for breeding purposes this year,
4) itu ud XXX-ba-ni
   (on the) thirtieth day of (the) month

REVERSE

1) ki--(?)-ni-ni-ni--ta
   by (?)ninini
2) ba-zig
   was delivered
3) itu ezen me-ki-gal
   (in the) month (of the) festival (of) Mekigal
4) mu bad mar-tu ba-ru(KAK)
   (in the) year (when the) western wall was built

SEAL

'he seal is only partly legible; but is evidently identical with
at which appears on XXIX, q. v.)

bv. 2: *dug* = *qabu* (*Br. 531*) = speak, etc. (*M-A. p. 902.*)
mu-gub. mu = year (*OBTR. p. 3 of Sign List*).   *gub* = stand,
c. (*MSL. p. 157*).

im (or *lum*) = fructification, fruit, growth, etc. (*MSL. p. 181*).

XXV

OBVERSE

) [   ] gud še šig
* * * * * fattened oxen, fine quality

) [   ] gud še šig uš
* * * * * fattened oxen, good quality

) VII gud še III-kam uš
7 fattened oxen, third quality

) III gud še IV-kam uš
3 fattened oxen, fourth quality

5) XXXV gud še
35 fattened oxen

6) XVII gud u(ŠAM)
17 pastured oxen

7) [   ] gud mu III
* * * * * oxen three years old

8) [gu]d amar ga
* * * * * suckling bull-calves

9) [   ] àb u(ŠAM)
* * * * * pastured cows

10) [   ] àb mu II
* * * * * cows two years old

11) [   ] àb amar ga
* * * * * suckling cow-calves

12) [   ] udu še šig
* * * * * fattened sheep, fine quality

13) [ga]nam še šig
    * * * * * *fattened ewes, fine quality*
14) [bir]-gal še šig
    * * * *fattened he-goats, fine quality*
15) [cu]-qar še šig
    * * * *fattened goat-heifers, fine quality*
16) [udu or ganam še] šig uš
    [* * **sheep or ewes] fattened, good quality*

Column II

1) V bir-gal še šig uš
    5 fattened he-goats, good quality
2) II cu-qar še šig uš
    2 fattened goat-heifers, good quality
3) XXIII udu še III-kam uš
    23 fattened sheep, third quality
4) XII bir-gal še III-kam uš
    12 fattened he-goats, third quality
5) I(?) cu-qar še III-kam uš
    1(?) fattened goat-heifer, third quality
6) XC udu še IV-kam uš
    90 fattened sheep, fourth quality
7) IX bir-gal še IV-kam uš
    9 fattened he-goats, fourth quality
8) V cu-qar še IV-kam uš
    5 fattened goat-heifers, fourth quality
9) CLVII udu še
    157 fattened sheep
10) X ganam še
    10 fattened ewes
11) LIII bir-gal še
    53 fattened he-goats
12) CCIV udu še gud-e uš-sa
    204 fattened sheep, stall-fed

3) XXXVI bir-gal še gud-e uš-sa
   36 *fattened he-goats, stall-fed*
4) XXIV sil še
   24 *fattened lambs*
5) VII sal-sil še
   7 *fattened she-lambs*

(REVERSE) Column III

1) IV bir še
   4 *fattened kids*
2) XXVI cu-qar še
   26 *fattened goat-heifers*
3) CCCXIX udu u(ŠAM)
   319 *pastured sheep*
4) LXIV bir-gal u(ŠAM)
   64 *pastured he-goats*
5) XCVIII ganam u(ŠAM)
   98 *pastured ewes*
6) LXVI uz u(ŠAM)
   66 *pastured goats*
7) XXXIII sil gab
   33 *weaned lambs*
8) XXVII sal-sil gab
   27 *weaned she-lambs*
9) VII bir gab
   7 *weaned kids*
10) XIII cu-qar gab
    13 *weaned she-kids*
11) VIII sil ga
    8 *suckling lambs*
12) III sal-sil ga
    3 *suckling she-lambs*

Column IV

1) [   ]LVII gud
   * * *57 *oxen*

51

2)   [   ]MCCCLX(?) udu
      * * 1360 (?) *sheep*

3)   [   ] la a
      * * * * *?* --- *?*

4)   [ki-]-ᵈen-lil-zi-ša(LIB)-gal(IK)--ta
      from Enlil-zišagal

5)   [a?]-xu-pi-ir ni-ku
      [*A?*]*xupir (being the) shepherd*

6)   [itu] maš-ru-kú ba-ni
      in (the [month] of) Mašruku

7)   [mu] uš-sa ᵈšu-ᵈen-
      [*in the year*] *after (the) divine Gimil-Sin,*

8)   [-zu] lugal uru-abᵏⁱ-ma-ge
      (*the*) *king of Ur,*

9)   [b]ad mar-tu mu-
      (*the*) *western* [*wall*], *Mu-*

10) [ri]-iq-ti-id-
      [*r*]*iq-tid-*

11) [ni]-im mu-ru
      [*n*]*im, built*

Col. IV. 7–11: "In the year after the divine Gimil-Sin, the king of Ur, built the western wall, Muriq-tidnim." See *Thureau-Dangin: Rec. Trav. XIX, p. 186*, and *F. A. Vanderburgh, JBL, 1913.*

In connection with this tablet see special note on classification of animals, Part I, § 10.

XXVI

OBVERSE

1)   MD še gun(TIG)
      1500 *gun (of) wheat*

2)   gi-zi(g)
      exact measure

3)   id ud itu mu ša(g)-ci
      portions (for) daily, monthly (and) yearly free-will offerings

=) ša-gal udu-še--šu(KU)
food for fattened sheep
5) ki--sukkal-max--ta
from (the) chief messenger
5) mu-gub
on hand

REVERSE

1) nu-ur-^dim
Nur-Im
2) šu-ba-ti
has received
3) gir lu-ka-ni
(the) overseer (being) Lukani
4) itu maš-ru-kù
(in the) month (of) Mašruku
5) mu en ^dnina uruk^{ki}-
(in the) year (when the) high-priest (of) Nina of Erech
6) -ga bir-e ni-pad
uttered the decision (oracle)

Rev. 6: *ga*, genitive suffix. *bir* (also read *maš*) = decision
(*OBTR*. p. 4, lines 7–8 and p. 17 of *Sign-List*) = oracle (*LSG*.
p. 150, line 5). -*e*, status rectus. *pad* = *tamû* = to speak, etc.

XXVII

OBVERSE

1) III udu u(ŠAM)
3 *pastured sheep*
2) šu-pu e(BIT)-mu
collected (at the) public kitchen
3) mu--ku-uš-e-ne--šu
intended for (the) officers
4) eri-mu pa-kabar
Erimu (being the) great official
5) III udu
3 *sheep*

6) zig-ga lugal
   expended (for the) king
7) IV ganam u(ŠAM)
   4 *pastured ewes*
8) I bir-gal u(ŠAM)
   1 *pastured he-goat*
9) I uz u(ŠAM)
   1 *pastured goat*
10) I sil gab
    1 *weaned lamb*
11) ba-til(BE)
    slaughtered

REVERSE

1) VII udu
   7 *sheep*
2) ᵈdun-gi-uru-mu
   Dungi-urumu
3) šu-ba-an-ti
   has received them;
4) ud XII-kam
   (on the) twelfth day
5) ki--ur-azag-nun-na--ta
   by Urazagnunna
6) ba-zig
   (they) were expended
7) gir II xu-pi-qar-
   (the) two overseers (being) Xupiqar-
8) -àb-ra-ab-du
   -abrabdu
9) ša(U) dug-ga-šag-ud
   and Duggašagud
10) itu ezen (ᵈ)an-na
    (in the) month (of the) festival (of) Anna
11) mu en ᵈnina uruk^{ki}-ga
    (in the) year (when the) high-priest (of) Nina of Erech

2) bir-e ni-pad
uttered the decision(oracle)

X udu
10 *sheep*

ov. 2: *šu-pu* = *sanâqu*(*Br.* 7211) = press together, collect, etc.
M-A. p. 711).

mu. mu = burn (*See LSG. p. 229*).   Compare, "*kalamma*
u-dim mu-mu-meš" = they burn the land like fire " (*CT. XVI.*
, 20b).   Hence, *e-mu* = house of burning.

kuš = officer, probably connected with *kuš* = *pa-an* (*MSL.*
215).

): See Part I, § 10.
ev. 3: *šu-ba-an-ti.*   -*an*-, infixed object of verb.
): See note on XII, R, 4.
2: See note on XXVI, R, 5–6.

XXVIII

OBVERSE

I sil ba-ba-ti
1 *lamb* (*of*) *Babati*
I sil lugal-má-gúr-ri
1 *lamb* (*of*) *Lugalmagurri*
I sil u-dar-al-šu
1 *lamb* (*of*) *Udaralšu*
mu-gub lugal
on hand : *royal property*
in-ta-e(UD-DU)-a
Intaea
ni-ku
(*being the*) *shepherd*

REVERSE

gir nu-ur-^den-zu dup-sar
(*the*) *overseer* (*being*) *Nur-Enzu* (*the*) *scribe*

2) [ud] XXV-kam
   (*on the*) *twenty-fifth* [*day*]
3) [itu] ezen ᵈnin-a-su
   (*in the* [*month*] *of the*) *festival* (*of*) *Ninasu*
4) mu ᵈšu-ᵈen-zu
   (*in the*) *year* (*when the*) *divine Gimil-Sin,*
5) lugal uru-abᵏⁱ-ma-ge
   king of Ur,
6) ma-da za-ap-ša-li-
   (*the*) *land* (*of*) *Zapšali*
7) -ᵏⁱ mu-xul
   laid waste

EDGE

III udu
3 *sheep*

Obv. 2: *Lugalmagurri* was a man of considerable prominence
being both Patesi of Nippur and " Commander of the Fortress."
(*HSA. pp. 299, 301.*)

4–6: Of course these lines are susceptible of the reading: " On
hand; Lugal-intaea being the shepherd." But I have adopted
the translation here given, as well as the parallel passage XIV
R, 4–5, after comparison, and bearing in mind that Intaea and
Abbašagga (see XIV) are well-known names.

Rev. 1: *Nur-Enzu.* Part of this name is very indistinct. However, the reading is obtained by comparison with XXI, R, 5.

XXIX

OBVERSE

1) I anšu še
   1 *fattened ass*
2) I maš-ru(KAK)
   1 *gazelle*
3) ᵈen-lil
   (*for*) *Enlil*

56

) I siqqa-bar še
1 *fattened antelope*

5) I maš-ru(KAK)
1 *gazelle*

6) ᵈnin-lil
(*for*) *Ninlil*

7) ša(LIB) tum-ma-al
in Tummal

REVERSE

1) lugal-še-šu-ra
(*in charge of*) *Lugalšešura*

2) ud I-kam
(*on the*) *first day*

3) ki--dug(KA)-ga-li--ta
from Duggali

4) ba-zig
expended

5) itu ezen-ᵈdun-gi
(*in the*) *month* (*of the*) *festival* (*of*) *Dungi*

6) mu ᵈšu-ᵈen-zu
(*in the*) *year* (*when the*) *divine Gimil-Sin*

7) lugal uru-abᵏⁱ-ma-ge
king of Ur

8) ma-da za-ap-ša-li-
(*the*) *land* (*of*) *Zapšali*

9) -ᵏⁱ mu-xul
laid waste

EDGE

[IV]
[4]

SEAL

1) ᵈšu-ᵈen-zu
(*the*) *divine Gimil-Sin*

2) lugal lig-ga
mighty king

57

3) lugal uru-ab^ki-ma
   king of Ur
4) lugal an-ub-da tab-tab
   king (of) the four regions
5) ur-^ddun-gi
   Ur-Dungi
6) dub-sar
   scribe
7) du ur-^dxa-ni-
   son (of) Ur-Xani
8) nita-zu
   thy servant

Seal 4: " King of the Four Quarters (of the Universe)."

XXX

OBVERSE

1) III gud še
   3 *fattened oxen*
2) zig-ga lugal
   expended (to the) king
3) I udu še gud-e uš-sa
   1 *fattened sheep, stall-fed*
4) dub aš-ni-a
   (per) tablet (of) Ašnia
5) III udu dub lu-ša-ši
   3 *sheep (per) tablet (of) Lušaši*
6) ki--ur-šu-ga-šul-lu--ta
   from Uršugašullu

REVERSE

1) lu-^dnin-tu
   Lu-Nintu
2) šu-ba-an-ti
   has received them

) itu ezen ᵈme-ki-gal(IK)
   (in the) month (of the) festival (of) Mekigal
) mu ᵈi-bi-ᵈen-zu lugal
   (in the) year (when the) divine Ibi-Sin (became) king

SEAL

1) lu-ᵈnin-gir-su
   Lu-Ningirsu
2) dub-sar
   (the) scribe
3) du ur-ᵈdun-gi-
   son (of) Ur-Dungi-
4) -sar-bi-mu
   -sarbimu

Rev. 2: *šubanti:* Notice the infixed object.

: Mekigal here has the god-sign, contrary to the general usage
n these tablets.

PART III.

SIGN-LIST AND GLOSSARY

(The form of a sign which appears on these tablets is first given, followed by the form used in the Assyrian period. The principal authoriti
for this List are AL⁵, Br, BBW, MSL, and OBTR. A few special references ar
included. Characters occurring on seals are starred (*). The List is c
plete only for these thirty tablets.)

1) AŠ numeral 1 (see Part I,#5,Numerals)

2) GIR dagger

3)* GÍR

4) DINGIR god (determinative before divine nam
AN heaven,high; pronominal infix 3d pers
* an-ub-da region (quarter of the Universe)

5) MU name; year; fire,burn; verbal prefix
mu-xul,mu-gub,mu-ru (see XUL,GUB,RU)p't I,#
* mu . . . šu for (see Part I,#5,Preposition

6) ŠEŠ,URU
šeš-da zebu (TAD.p.8)
* uru-abᵏⁱ-ma city of Ur

7) NANNAR

8) TIL slaughter
ba-til slaughtered

9) NA pronominal suffix 3d pers.
na-ra-am (Sem.)beloved

10) TI receive
šu-ba-ti received (see Part I,#5,Verb)

11) BAL strong

12) NU

13) UZ goat

14) MUQ shabby,inferior

15) MAX great

16) NITA, UR(U), ERI servant,slave

*

60

17)   AK   make, do, etc.

18)   BAR, MAŠ
      maš-ru   gazelle

19)   MA
      ma-da   land, country
   * ma-na   a unit of weight or value (= 1/60 gun = 60 gin)

20)   DAR

21)   GAL, IK

22)   QIN

23)   EN   lord, high-priest
      en-lil   city of Nippur
   * ᵈen-zu   Sin (the moon-god)

24)   EN-ZU   (see above & 71)

25)   DINGIR-EN   (see 4 and 23)

26)   BIR (or MÁŠ)   kid; oracle (see Note on XXVII.R.6)
      bir-gal   he-goat (see Part I, #10)

27)   XU   bird

28)   LU   man
      lu-kabar (great man) an official
   *

29)   SIQQA   antelope, ibex
      siqqa-bar   some variety of above

30)   NINA or INNANNA   the goddess Ištar

31)   RI(G)

32)   GI   measure
      gi-ra   slaughtered (SAI, 1614)
   * gi-zi   exact measure (see below)

33)   ZI, ZIG, ZID   expend, pay; exact (see above)
      ba-zig, zig-ga   expended, paid

34)   NAM   prefix of abstract
      nam-šid   priesthood

35)   MA   ship
      ma-du-du   skipper

36)   NUN
      nun^ki   city of Eridu

61

37)		ŠUŠŠANA	one-third
38)		TAB	numeral 2 (see Part I,#5,Numerals)
39)*		TAB-TAB numeral 4	tab-tab-ba
40)	(?)	TUR (or KUD)	
41)		GAB	ground grain,meal(see P't I,#10) dedicate,etc. ba-ab-gab dedicate put forth (in qa-šu-gab q.v.)
42)		GUD	ox,bull gud-e uš-sa stalled cattle(see P't I,#10)
43)		AM	
44)		UM	mother
45)		DUK	pot,vessel
46)		QAR	(in CU-QAR q.v.)
47)		PA	official pa-kabar lit."great official" pa-te-si ruler of a city pa-al seer
48)		PA-AL	(see above & 142)
49)		GUR	a measure of capacity (=300 qa)
50)		MAR mar-tu	the West (see Note on IX,0,5)
51)		UD ud-šar	day new moon
52)		E (UD-DU)	
53)		NER,NIR	hero,prince
54)		I	
55)		ŠU	hand; favor,grace(Ass.gimlu); verbal prefix (see P't I,#5,V'b)
*		šu-ba-ti,šu-ba-an-ti (see TI) šu-pu gathered	
56)		GAL,KAL	great
57)		DA	suffix(see Part I,#5,Prepositions)
*			

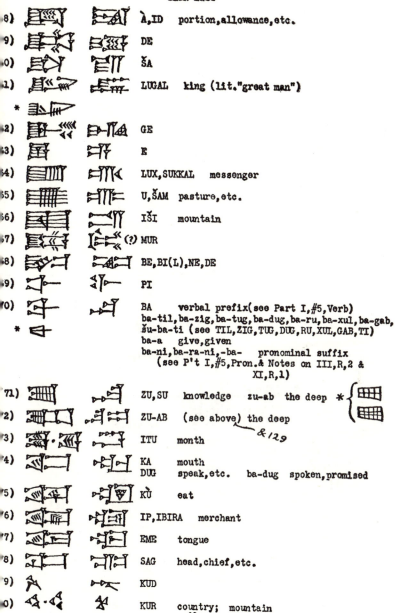

58) À,ID portion,allowance,etc.

59) DE

60) ŠA

61) LUGAL king (lit."great man")

*

62) GE

63) E

64) LUX,SUKKAL messenger

65) U,ŠAM pasture,etc.

66) IŠI mountain

67) (?) MUR

68) BE,BI(L),NE,DE

69) PI

70) BA verbal prefix(see Part I,#5,Verb)
     ba-til,ba-zig,ba-tug,ba-dug,ba-ru,ba-xul,ba-gab,
     šu-ba-ti (see TIL,ZIG,TUG,DUG,RU,XUL,GAB,TI)
*   ba-a give,given
     ba-ni,ba-ra-ni,-ba- pronominal suffix
       (see P't I,#5,Pron.& Notes on III,R,2 &
                                    XI,R,1)

71) ZU,SU knowledge zu-ab the deep *

72) ZU-AB (see above) the deep
                              &129

73) ITU month

74) KA mouth
    DUG speak,etc. ba-dug spoken,promised

75) KÙ eat

76) IP,IBIRA merchant

77) EME tongue

78) SAG head,chief,etc.

79) KUD

80) KUR country; mountain

63

81) XUM,LUM   fruit,plenty,increase,breeding
a-lum   fruitfulness
lum-za   plenty-of-jewels

82) DUN,ŠUL   man,lord
dun-mal-a   an official(lord-of-the-house)
*

83)* UB   region,etc.

84) QA   a measure of capacity(=1/300 gur)
qa-šu-gab   grain-measurer (see Note on XI

85) RU,DU   build,make
mu-ru he built   ba-ru it was built

86) NI,ZAL   verbal prefix   ni-pad (see PAD)
NI-NI   plural idiogram for dingir(god),As
*   ni-ku   shepherd   (
-ni   3d pers.pl.termination

87) IR

88) GU
ᵍⁱˢgu-za   throne

89) AX

90) TE,TEMEN   receive
te-te   received   temen-na   received

91) KAM   determinative used after numerals
employed like copular verb(see Not
V,

92) IM

93) QAR
qar-zi-da   an epithet of Nannar

94) LUL

95) GIR   overseer

96) ANŠU   ass

97) SA,DI
sa-dug   regular offering,tribute

98) KI   place (determinative after place-n
ki . . . ta   from(see Part I,#5,Preps.)
*   ki-lal   weight,value
ki-sig   couch

64

99)		AZAG	brightness, silver
100)		ŠA(G)	heart; used as preposition in
		ša-ci	free-will offering
		ša-gal	food
101)		U	numeral 10
102)		ÀB	cow
103)		GIG	night, darkness
104)		NIŠ	numeral 20
105)		UŠU	numeral 30
106)		ŠI	eye
107)		ŠIG	purified, clean, etc.
108)		PAD	speak, declare ni-pad declared
109)		UX(U)	
110)		ŠA,U	and
		ša-a	old, elderly
111)		XUL	evil; lay waste, destroy
			ba-xul it was destroyed mu-xul he destroyed
112)		PU,BU	
113)		AMAR	calf, young, offspring (Ass.bur)
114)		SIGIŠŠE	offering pl:sigišše-sigišše
115)		XAR,GUR,MUR	command, *decree*
116)		NIMIN	numeral 40
117)		ŠE	wheat; fattened (see Note on II,0,1);
118)		IN	*a measure of weight or value* (= $1/_{180}$ gin)
119)		TU(R)	
120)		LI	
121)		ALIM (supplied in XIX,R,3)	
122)		ŠAR,SAR	brightness; fullness

*⯗⯗⯗

123) DARA   antelope; ibex

124) GIŠ   wood (determinative used before
          articles of wood, implements e
   giš-eme "tongue-wood"(Lau)
   giš-ur   beams (see Note on IV,0,3) (see U
   ^{giš}gu-za throne

125) SI

126) GUB   be present, etc.   mu-gub on hand
   DU   to be, etc.
   GIN

127) KABAR, RIM   great, large

128) UR

129) AB   house; temple; pronominal infix
                        (P't I,#5,Pro
   *

130) URUK   uruk^{ki} city of Erech

131) CI

132) GUN   a measure of value or weight (=60 ma

133) BI   pronominal suffix 3d pers.(P't I,#5,
   *

134) TA   locative suffix; (used alone) from
   ki . . . ta from (see Part I,#5,Prepositio

135) GA   milk; genitive suffix(see P't I,#
   *

136) URU   city

137) EZEN   feast, festival

138) BAD   wall

139) TUM, IB
   ib-ra   an official

140) UŠ   to stand; grade, quality
   III-kam uš   third quality
   uš-sa "standing bound"
   gud-e uš-sa stalled cattle
   mu uš-sa   the year after
   uš-sa lugal   belonging to the king

uš-bar   weaver

141)   AD   father

142)   AL

143)   GAN, XE

   *

144)   ĐUB   tablet
         dub-sar   scribe
   *   e-dub-ba   house of records

145)   LA

146)   ĜAL, MAL   house;   to be

147)   GAN

148)   SIL   lamb

149)   UR   enclosure

150)   KALAM, UKU   people (determinative before tribes)

151)   KAL, LIG   great, mighty   lig-ga
   *

152)   ŠID   priest   nam-šid   priesthood(see NAM)

153)   RA   motion (see Note on III,R,2)

154)   RA-NI   (see 153 & 86)

155)   SAL   female   sal-sil   she-lamb

156)   CU-QAR   goat-heifer (young female)

157)   GEME   female slave

158)   NIN   lady, priestess
   *

159)   DAM

160)*   DU, TUR   son

161)   XUL   (in UDU-XUL & GANAM-XUL q.v.)
            joy (see Note on IX,O,1)

162)   DIŠ   numeral 1 (see Part I,#5,Numerals)
         GEŠ   numeral 60

163) MIN numeral 2 or 120 (see P't I,#5,Num

164) EŠ numeral 3 or 180

165) LIMMU numeral 4 or 240

166) IA numeral 5 or 300

167) AŠŠA numeral 6 or 360

168) IMIN numeral 7 or 420

169) USSU numeral 8 or 480

170) ME

171) ME-KI (see 170 & 98)

172) NER numeral 600

173) ŠA,GAR cut,etc.
       ša-su property

174) NIGIN (ŠA-E)? sunrise

175) UR dog (used frequently in personal na
       in the sense of "servant" or "worsh
   * ⊔ per"of a divinity)

176) LAL loss,minus,etc.
       ten-LAL-one=nine(P't I,#5,Numerals)
    (⊢ LAL-I)

177) GIN a measure of weight or value(=180 ŝ
                                        =1/60 mana

178) NIGIN fulness,etc.
       nigin-ru perfect (see Note on IX,0,2)

179) KU garment
       ku-uš-e-ne officers

180) TUG,KU establish,place,etc.
       ba-an-tug,ba-tug established,enacted,etc.

181) ŠU (KU) (suffix) for ⎛180 &181 are use
                            ⎝ interchangeab

182) UDU sheep
       LU

183) UDU-XUL fine sheep (see 183 & 161)

184) SIG wool a-sig woolliness

185) GANAM ewe

186) GANAM-XUL   fine ewe (see 185 & 161)

187) SA   bind

188) E   house, temple
     e-mu   bakery (h'se of burning--see 5)
     e-kal   palace (great house--see 56)
     e-ku   refectory (h'se of eating--see 75)
     LIL   wind; demon; land
     GE   genitive suffix (see P't I,#5,Prep$)

189) ŠAG   pure, good, etc.
     -šag-ga   element used in proper names
     * (?)

190) A   water; (suffix) for; abstract prefix
     a-ši or ER   tear (see 106) (Note on V,R,8)
     a-du   time
     a-sìg   woolliness (see P't I,#5,Noun)
     a-lum   fruitfulness

191) ZA   jewel; a by-form of numeral 4 (see 165)

192) XA
     *

69

ALPHABETICAL INDEX TO SIGN–LIST

PART IV

PLATES

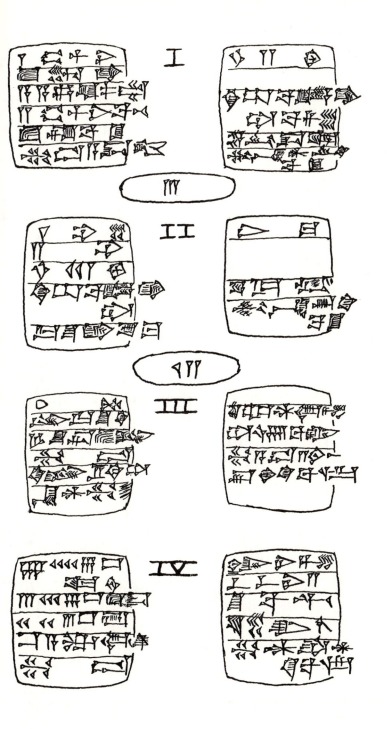

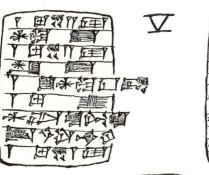 V

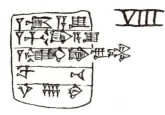

 VI

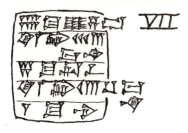

VII

VIII

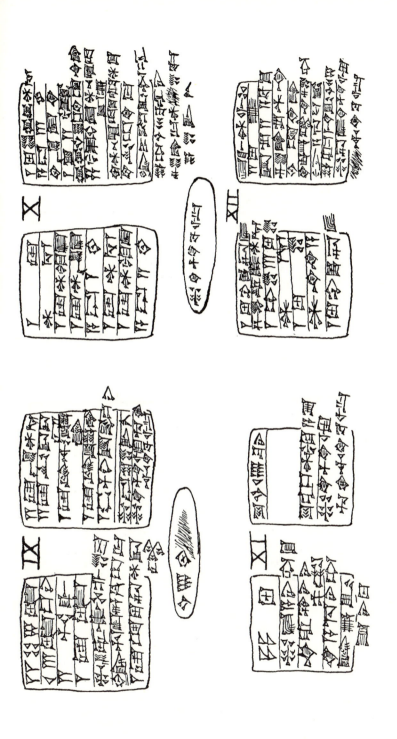

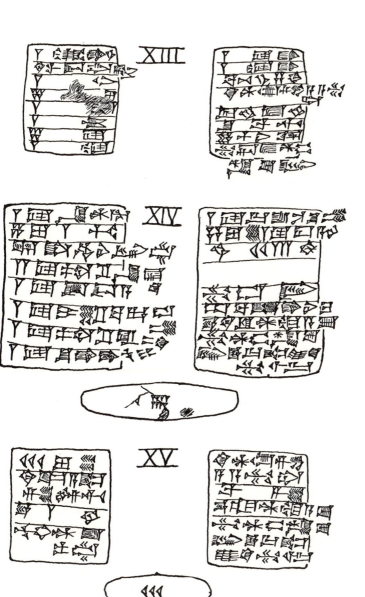

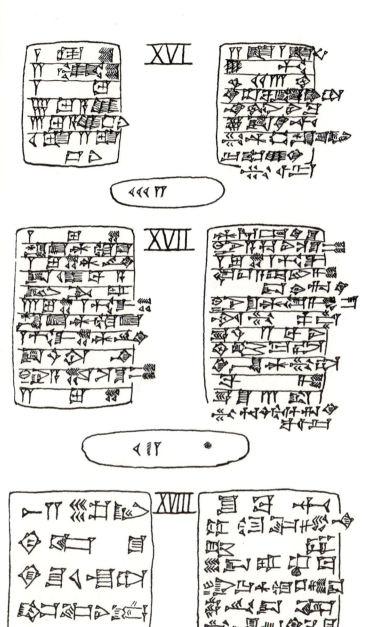

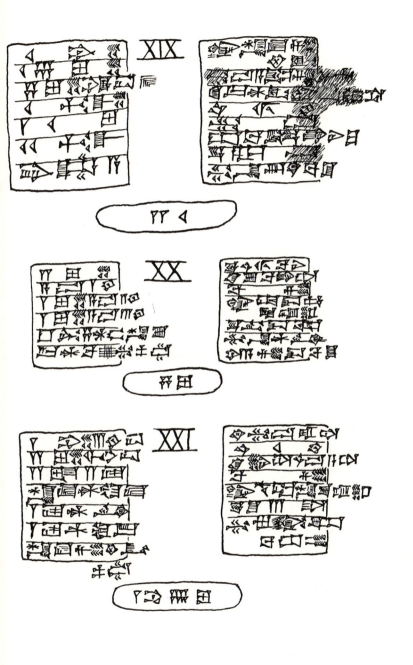

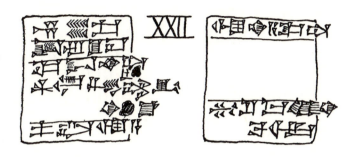

XXII

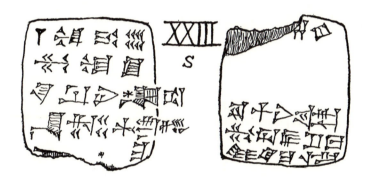

XXIII

S

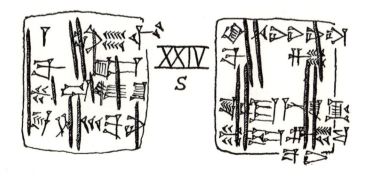

XXIV

S

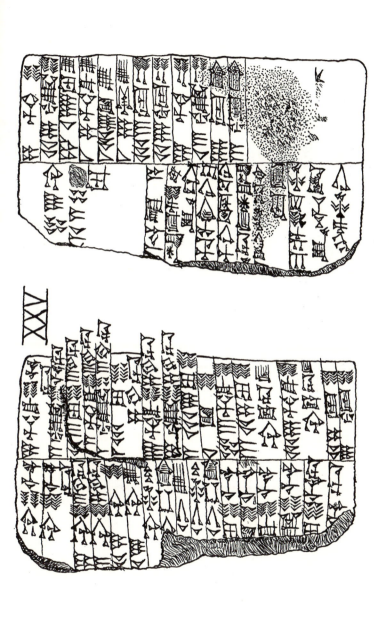

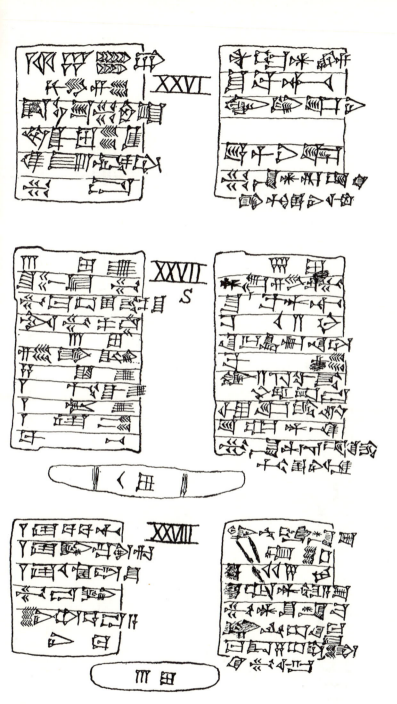

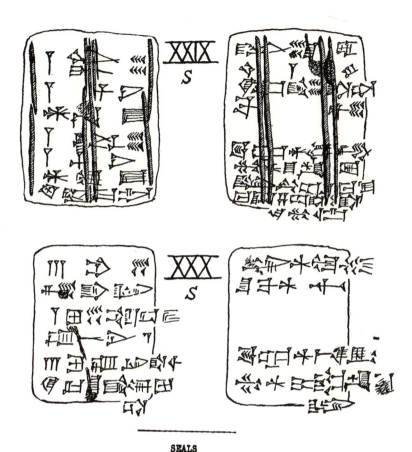

XXIX

S

XXX

S

SEALS
(enlarged four times)

XXIV and XXIX

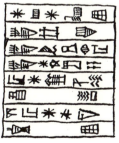

XXIII

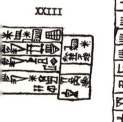

XXX